BISEXUAL LIVING

Bisexual Living

by JULIUS FAST
(author of BODY LANGUAGE)
& HAL WELLS, Ph.D.

Including an interview
with Wardell B. Pomeroy
co-author with Alfred C. Kinsey
of *Sexual Behavior in the
Human Male*

M. Evans and Company, Inc.
NEW YORK, NEW YORK 10017

The heterosexual-homosexual rating scale that appears on page 229 is reprinted from *Sexual Behavior in the Human Male* by Alfred C. Kinsey, et al. Reprinted by permission of the Institute for Sex Research.

M. Evans and Company titles are distributed in the United States by the J. B. Lippincott Company, East Washington Square, Philadelphia, Pa. 19105 and in Canada by McClelland & Stewart Ltd., 25 Hollinger Road, Toronto M4B 3G2, Ontario

Library of Congress Cataloging in Publication Data

Fast, Julius, 1918-
  Bisexual living.

  1. Bisexuality—Case studies.

  I. Wells, Hal
joint author. II. Title.
HQ74.F37   1975   301.41'5   74-30475
ISBN 0-87131-172-0

Contents

A NOTE TO THE READER

With Dr. Hal Wells, a clinical psychologist, I located hundreds of bisexuals throughout the country, talked to them and eventually selected ten to interview. The interviews are all presented as taking place at one time. Very few did. In most cases many sessions were necessary to draw out the facts, and because space was a serious consideration, only those facts that seemed relevant were kept.

Dr. Wells has studied each interview, and has analyzed the subjects to explain the reasons for their behavior. His analysis follows each interview.

—Julius Fast

1
A Visit to a Social

"BISEXUAL LIBERATION is pleased to announce a super party-dance with live music this Friday at 7:30 with a big surprise addition. Contribution $3.50."

The place is on 73rd Street, between Second and Third Avenues, a rambling brick building with four small theaters, and when I get there, the shows are letting out and I have to make my way in against a stream of people coming out. None look bisexual, but what does a real bisexual look like? Some are my age, some are kids in jeans and workshirts. I see a sign for the Burlap Room in the basement and try it, but a play is going on there, and in spite of the usher's earnest invitation to come in, I back away.

I try upstairs, and on the second floor there's a small table, outside one of the meeting rooms, with a cashbox and some papers, but no sign to tell me what's going on in the room. I wander into a darkened hall with chairs around the sides. About ten people are sitting there, some are couples, but most are single men. Each has taken a seat a chair away from his neighbor.

There's a light box on a table against one wall, and it sends out intermittent blue and red flashes. Some bottles of liquor, soda, and Coke and a few cups crowd out a bowl of potato chips on the table. I sit down uneasily and let my eyes adjust to the dim light. Across the room a handsome young black man with a beard catches my eye and smiles. I nod, and look away quickly to find myself staring at two heavyset men on the chairs next to me.

Awkwardly, I stand up and move around the room, over to the table with the light box, then to the doorway. A young man is at the outside table now, and he looks up as I come out. I take my courage in hand and ask, "Is this where the Bisexual Liberation group meets?"

He looks a bit pained. "We're Bi-Lib. Do you want to sign in?" He's close to thirty, a trimmed beard and mustache covering his round, acne-scarred face. He fills out his jeans and denim jacket, stocky but not fat.

I hesitate over signing in, then shrug, what the hell, and I put my real name down. He says, "That'll be three-fifty for the social and a drink. Other drinks are a buck, only we're short on cups." He looks at my name and nods. "You're the body language man. I'm Don Fass."

We joke about the similar names, and then I ask him how the group got started. "It's my baby," he tells me. "I organized it as a social way for bisexuals to meet. Usually we meet at my place, but sometimes we get together like this. There was going to be a play-reading and music and dancing, but the musicians—they were going to read the play, too— never showed."

A young woman saunters out, her hands in her pants pockets. She wears sneakers, a T-shirt, and a worn man's jacket. She walks and stands like a man. "Hey, like I think I ought to get a refund. There's no music here."

Nervously, Don counts out $3.50 and hands it to her. "It's usually not like this. We expected a lot of people, but the *Village Voice* forgot our ad—I don't know how they did it, but they did."

Another young man with a reddish beard, good-looking and with a quick, easy smile, comes out, and a young girl follows him. She's twenty or twenty-one, small and slim and exceptionally pretty. She, too, wears a jacket, a thrift-shop special, and she brushes her dark hair back. "How about a refund?"

Don takes a firm stand. "I can't give any refunds." Then, vaguely, "There's no cash left."

The girl thinks for a minute. "Then how about a rain check?"

"Sure." Don scribbles something on a slip and hands it to her. "Next Friday at that address."

She goes off with the red-bearded young man and Don shakes his head. "If only the band came."

I pull a chair to the table and the two of us sit down outside the room. "Have you always been bisexual?" I ask.

"No. I was straight—heterosexual—until a few years ago. Then I needed a roommate to save on expenses, and I began to realize that the guys who answered my ad were looking for sex, too. I think at that point, though I didn't admit it to myself, I knew what was going to happen. I found a guy who was young and good-looking and took him in as a roommate, then I arranged things so that the whole place was too cluttered. We had to share a bed."

"How did you do that?" I try to keep the disbelief out of my voice.

"I managed." He's disarmingly vague. "I didn't sleep for a couple of nights, and finally he asked me what was wrong.

I said, 'I think I want sex with you,' and he said, 'Well, O.K.,' and that was it."

"Do you still feel interested in women?" I ask.

Don frowns. "I don't feel that the life experience of the bisexual is against people of the opposite sex. I just feel it's adding an experience. Look, we're turning to, not away from, people."

"But why?"

"Well, most of us have had good sexual experiences with women, and we don't see why our sex life should be restricted to women—so we add men. I'm sure it's the same way with women. You know, most people, in my experience, get into bisexuality by accident. A lot come in through swinging couples. They find that swinging isn't satisfying because it doesn't lead to any lasting relationships—and that's our intention."

"How do the others come to it?"

"Well, a lot get in through experimental groups, encounter groups that involve touching and feeling. They find that touching another man isn't half as threatening as they thought it would be."

A tall, heavy man comes out of the room. "You got any cups here?"

"We're low. Hey, Jim!" Don calls, and a teen-age boy comes out. "You wanna go out and see if you can get some cups?" Don gives him a dollar.

We're alone again, and I ask, "Were you afraid of men?"

"I was, but not anymore. I also found my fear of men wasn't only in the sexual area. It was generalized. You know—." Scowling, he chews his lower lip. "If you're a swinger, which everyone thinks all bisexuals are, you gotta put in a lot of planning. Couples get together, they have to match the right people—all that stuff. We're not after that. We want a relationship with one sex or the other, or both at the same time. Basically, you know, I think swingers are chauvinistic—it's okay for the women but not for the men. Men don't usually have any sex with each other in swinging."

Confused, I say, "Straighten me out. Don't you have that in bisexuality?"

"Well, often there's an agreement, a kind of noninterference pact. Let's say the wife wants to swing with a woman, but she agrees not to have sex with a man because it might threaten her husband, and vice versa. There seems to be no feeling of competition with the same sex.

"And another thing. Bisexuality seems to eliminate sex roles. You can act out either role, and understand the man or woman—depending on which role you're acting, or you can put the roles aside and be yourself. You know, most men feel threatened by doing women's jobs. Once they get into a bisexual relationship with another man, this tends to be less threatening. I'd say seventy per cent of bisexual men come from the straight world, from either marriage or long-term relationships with women."

Jim comes running back, taking the stairs two at a time. "Hey, man. There's no cups anywhere. It's too late. All the stores are closed."

Don takes the dollar back, frowning. "Yeah, well, we'll have to see." He turns back to me, trying to pick up the thread. "We bisexuals are looking for partners, and many more things besides sex. We know we can have many types of sexual relationships, but we want a deeper, interpersonal human reaction, so we don't restrict it to body sex."

"If not body sex, then what kind?"

"Well, it boils down to basic human values. We aim to get people back to primary relationships, not to be terrified of close emotions. You know, your bisexual is pretty much a square, and yet he's freer than the average gay person."

"Is bisexuality peculiar to the big cities?" I ask.

"Well, we have six chapters in large cities around the country, and we're expanding. Outside New York people are locked into their sex roles a lot less than they are here. In smaller cities, everyone knows each other. The same thing happens with bisexuals in small towns. They're a tightly knit circle. They don't have the hostility you find in the gay world, maybe because they aren't threatened by either sex."

"But you were afraid of men."

"I lost my fear of being gay when I became bisexual. I stopped focusing on the gay part of the relationship and focused on the human part. You know, the young people don't label our activities bisexual, just sexual. Also, the younger kids, nineteen and twenty, can act out their feelings with less threat than older ones, people in their thirties or older. Today, kids act out of choice, not social pressure."

"There seem to be more men here tonight than women. Is that typical?"

"No. In my experience, more women tend to be bisexual. Men talk about it a lot, but women seem to act it out. Also, there are bisexual preferences. Like a woman may be bisexual but prefer a man, or a man may prefer a man and swing both ways. You know, it's hard for a bisexual to say who his next partner will be, a man or a woman."

I nod. "Do many people come to your meetings?"

"Many?" He considers. "I'd say in the last two years over three thousand people have attended our meetings, and we receive about twenty thousand calls a year asking about them."

A black couple, young and attractive, come out and tell Don, "We're going. Sorry they didn't show up."

"Well, yeah. I'll see you again."

A thin man in his forties, well-dressed and fussily effeminate, comes out with a bottle. "Well, really. How are we supposed to drink?"

"We're short of cups." Don looks about uncertainly. "I thought I saw some in the other room."

I say, "I'll take a look," and I walk next door. There's a coffee maker and a pile of cups on a table, and a man and a woman are rehearsing a scene from a play. I interrupt to ask if I can borrow some cups, and they give me permission, then watch curiously as I walk out with them. Is it because I came from the Bi-Lib meeting?

Don thanks me and takes the cups, and I walk inside again. The room has livened up now, and there's a circle of eight men and women in one corner and a group around the liquor table. The light box has stopped flashing, but the room is still comfortably dim, almost dark. Two men are standing against the wall with drinks, the fussy one and another, tall and bald. While I pour myself a Coke, I see them casually reach down and grope each other. Embarrassed, I turn away, and find the young black man with the beard standing next to me.

He smiles shyly and asks, "Is this your first visit?"

I say, "Yes. Is it yours?"

"My first one. I don't know many people here in the city and this is a way to find someone, isn't it?" He has a curious accent, partly British and partly Jamaican, and properly so. He tells me his father came from Jamaica and his mother was English. "White, my mother. I grew up in England, but they used to send me to Jamaica to visit my grandparents."

"And what are you doing over here?"

"I'm a graduate student at Columbia. I'm studying business administration. I don't know. I thought it would only be for a while, but I like New York."

We move away and sit down in two chairs against the wall while he tells me about himself. The point at which I can explain that I am only here as a researcher has passed, so I let him assume I too am here looking—for what? Friendship? A sexual encounter?

"How long have you been bisexual?" I ask.

"Oh, not long. A few years ago, at a family party, I met my mother's lawyer. We fell in love and it was very wonderful. He had his own flat."

"Were there girls before then?"

"Oh, yes, before and after. Now I live with relatives uptown and I have my own room—I pay twenty-five dollars a week—but it is hard to bring girls there and impossible to bring men."

"What did you hope to find here tonight?"

He looks around and smiles rather sadly. "Someone to be a friend, to understand. Perhaps a lover, but if not, a friend."

"A woman?"

He is a bit startled. "I was only thinking in terms of a man, but I suppose a woman, too—." Gesturing vaguely at the others, he says, "I think what I really want is a man. Not a gay man, but a married man, a man with children—really a man."

"But what kind of relationship could you have with someone like that?" I ask, puzzled.

He smiles and shrugs. "A safe one, for one thing. But here, most of these men are gay and looking for the same thing."

"Then why come here? Why not try a gay bar or some cruising spot?"

"You'll only find gay men there. We come here perhaps because a bisexual is a little more of a man."

"But you are bisexual, too, aren't you?"

"Yes . . ." There is a long pause. "And I want to meet a bisexual man. Are you married?"

Startled, I nod.

"And you have children?"

"Yes." I look at my watch. "I didn't realize it was that late. I have to get going."

He nods. "I must get to work early tomorrow. I'll go, too." He picks up his briefcase and hesitates. "Can I give you my phone number?"

I nod and he writes it down, smiles shyly, and leaves. I have another Coke for a dollar, say good-bye to Don, and leave, too, the social now in full swing, the light box flickering again.

2
Bill and Lisa

The housing project lies outside Queens proper, a bus ride from the last subway stop. The buildings are twenty-five years old, built quickly after World War II and kept poorly for the past ten years. It's a large complex of two-story buildings, all joined together with a border of trampled grass in front and back. The grass gives them the right to be called garden apartments.

Bill and Lisa live in a two-bedroom apartment on the second floor. Their living room is crowded with an overwhelming modern red-plush couch with ornate wooden arms. The coffee table in front of it is a gaudy elaboration of gilt, glass, and carved wood. The rest of the room is shabby, the shades torn, the corners piled with a clutter of children's toys and boxes, bicycles and carriages. The buff paint on the stairway and walls is peeling and old.

A huge German shepherd growls menacingly as I walk in,

but Bill shouts an angry command and it slinks reluctantly to its place in the corner. During our talk it comes forward gingerly, turning its head at Bill's stern orders, but persisting like a wayward child until it eventually wins out and lies down at my feet near the table.

For a while we talk about dogs to ease our initial embarrassment, until Lisa says, brusquely, "You didn't come just to talk dogs, did you?"

Bill offers me beer and I accept eagerly. When he brings it in, he sits down with a grin. "This reminds me of the time Lisa and I went to a gay bar looking for another woman. I was just as embarrassed as you are now. I thought it would be mixed gay, but it was all men. I couldn't meet anyone's eye." He laughs. "We just finished our drinks and got up to leave and a guy sitting at this table says right out loud, 'He's kind of fat'!

"His friend looks at me and says, 'Yes, but he's cute.' I started to get red all over my face. I suddenly realized what it's like to be a sex object."

Bill laughs and his belly shakes. Just thirty, he's a short, pudgy man with the remnants of a boyish face marred by encroaching fat. Through his open shirt his breasts hang over a paunchy stomach, and the fat seems to have spread around to his back.

Lisa is overweight, too, but she still has traces of prettiness. Her hair is short and blonde, and since she's wearing pants and a sweater, it's hard to tell just how much poundage she carries. She's close to Bill's age, but quieter, more observant, and for all Bill's blustering, she runs the show.

Now that the ice is broken, Bill plunges into his own story. Where I had anticipated some embarrassment, there is none. Bill doesn't have to be drawn out. He wants to talk, almost compulsively needs to. He's been having trouble on his job, a training program for a television-repair firm. This is supposed to be his last week on the job, but he's certain he can talk his supervisor into keeping him on.

I ask him what started the whole job problem.

"A disbelief in my own abilities and in myself as a human being. It made me afraid and insecure, insecure of my wife's love." He looks at Lisa and smiles, and she smiles back, a warm, intimate exchange. "Her love is something I should never doubt," he says slowly and deliberately, "because she stuck with me through hell. Very few women would have stuck with their husbands through what she did."

"What was the problem?" I ask.

"Basically, my own insecurity, my own hang-ups. I confessed all of them one night last December. I laid everything on the line to her. We had an argument going, and I finally yelled at her, she wouldn't understand.

"She said, 'How am I supposed to if you don't tell me?' So we sat down and I got everything out, everything that was inside hurting and bothering me. You know, she understood everything, and lo and behold, a lot of things that were hang-ups just disappeared. When I got them out in the open, they just stopped bothering me. I could of kicked myself that I didn't do this ten years earlier."

"What kind of things?" I ask.

"Sexual hang-ups, fantasies—I guess there was a guilt complex, too. I got it all out and she understood everything. This is where our marriage is at right now." He pounded his knee with his fist for emphasis. "We have total honesty about everything, and we absolutely have no secrets from each other on anything—on any subject."

"Have you always been bisexual?"

He frowns a little. "Well—yes. Not out of any desire for a man," he adds quickly. "What I needed was a man's attention and affection, which I never got from my father. My father never paid any attention to me except to say, 'Go

wash the dishes—Go change your brother—Is supper ready?' "
He shakes his head. "I had four brothers. I'm the oldest."

Nudging him back, I ask, "What were your bisexual experiences like?"

"I played a passive role. I'd stand there and let them
fellate me, just for the attention. That's all I wanted, the
attention." He sips his beer, frowning, and Lisa sits quietly,
smiling at him. I'm struck by her ability to stay motionless,
not talking or moving, almost a part of the gaudy couch.

"My mother fooled around before my father died," Bill
says. "I really didn't give a shit because I wasn't that wild
on my father to begin with, but I didn't want her neglecting
me because of it. I'd be left watching the kids when I was
eight or nine while she was out fooling around with my
father's best friend. She was a closet alcoholic!"

He pauses, and then, as if reading from some unseen
manual in a suddenly neutral voice, says, "This caused me to
have a distrust of women which I carried over into my marriage. Right, Hon?"

Lisa moves, and for the first time indignation comes into
her voice. "Well, I hate to be lying in bed fast asleep and
have you come rushing in to accuse me of doing something."

Bill nods. "I would daydream that she was having an affair
with somebody. Right at work I'd dream it, and I'd come
rushing home to catch her with her lover, and I'd find her
washing the dishes or doing the wash. I'd be all set to play
the part of an outraged husband, and I'd find I'm a jerk,
a dummy. I'd have this groundless, stupid distrust, a petty
jealousy my wife didn't deserve. I worked that out, maybe
not one hundred per cent but ninety-five."

I look at Lisa's tender smile and ask, "How old were you
when you first met?"

Bill says, "Sixteen?" with a questioning look at Lisa. She
nods, and he chuckles. "I was going steady with her best

friend. When we split up, I didn't see her or the old crowd for a while, but then I was going into the Navy, and I got together with the old crowd to say good-bye, and Lisa was there and I walked her home. We started making out in front of her door, and then we went inside—but we didn't go all the way. I saw her every day that week, and then in boot camp I still kept telling her how much I loved her, but I didn't really believe it—well, maybe I half-believed it because I needed someone."

Lisa laughs and brushes her hair back. "I didn't believe a word of it. He gives me this ring and says, 'Keep it for me.' I tell him I don't want a ring, and he says, 'Just keep it, just hold it!' "

Bill shrugs. "I was just seventeen, and I wasn't sure what I wanted. But when I got out of boot camp and was stationed in Brooklyn I gave her a real engagement ring. The chemistry was there all of a sudden. Everything was right. You know, Lisa was the first woman I ever made love to?"

"What about men?"

Bill shrugs this off. "Yes, but she was the first woman. Before that I always used to fantasize about what kind of woman I liked. It wasn't Lisa."

Smiling, Lisa says, "Thanks."

"No, listen. My ideal woman, the one I would fantasize about, she was a Jewish woman of about thirty-five or forty, very elegant, very chic, sophisticated. Not very heavily made-up, but eye make-up, rings, a nice pantsuit, driving a Cadillac—that's my ideal."

There's a long silence, and then Bill says, "I went through a very emotional period five years ago. I just completely withdrew into myself. We went on welfare and moved here. I'd lose one job after another or I'd quit. It was a very trying period." Shaking his head, he looks at Lisa. "My wife has to love me an awful lot to have stayed with me through that. It was hell for her, really hell. She had to be the head of the family all by herself. She couldn't count on me. I found a corner of my mind and just hid there.

"It took a while for me to get out of that, and it wasn't until I faced the truth about myself. I wanted to fail, honest to God, I wanted it. I think the hardest thing I ever did in my whole life was to face that truth. Anything else I've ever done, facing a machine gun in Vietnam, fighting a man twice my size, entering the ring as an amateur boxer—hell, those things were nothing next to facing the truth about myself. That took guts. That was a turning point!"

His voice is charged with emotion, and he lights a cigarette unsteadily. I ask him about the trouble with his job.

"I made mistakes. I made them purposely because I was getting too successful. It's the old business. I didn't deserve to be successful. I had to punish myself."

Carefully, I ask, "When did you come to grips with your life, realize all this? After your trouble on the job or before it?"

Frowning a little, as if trying to get the dates straight, Bill counts on his fingers. "It was—six months ago."

"That was when you unburdened yourself to your wife?"

He nods, looking quickly at Lisa. "It brought us much closer together. We have such a high degree of sharing now. We share everything, anything. We're like a couple of teen-agers going steady."

The trouble on the job is only a few weeks old, but I let this area alone. "What about the kids?" I ask. I know they have three children, but I've seen no sign of them except for the toys in the corner.

Reluctantly, Bill admits that the kids are a problem. "My son is a middle child and he's hyperactive, and my older daughter has an emotional problem—she's very self-centered. The baby's all right, but the two older ones are seeing a psychiatrist, a really caring woman who really cares about us . . ."

He lets this hang, considering the entire problem of the children, then he shakes his head as if clearing it away and returns to his own problem. "A few weeks ago I went through a real problem, a real crying jag where I broke down and spent the whole day just crying, in the car, in the restaurant . . ." He shakes his head in wonder.

"You know, crying's an unmasculine thing. God forbid that a man should cry, but ever since then I've felt like a pressure cooker with a release valve, as if the stopper came off and the excess steam blew out. Little things kept happening, one after another, and they led up to the final transition where I broke away from my old self and became really me."

There's a confusion of time here, and I try to sort it out. "This has been in the last few weeks?"

"That's right."

"But you worked things out with Lisa six months ago? Wasn't that what freed you?"

"Yes, sexually, but I still had hang-ups in my personality, on my job. These last six months have led up to this, to this crying jag. Now I'm a different man. I feel self-confident, almost cocky. Even if I lose my job, I'm going to make it."

I let this lie for the moment. "Let's talk about you and Lisa. How did the two of you get into the bisexual groove?"

"That was after I confessed everything to Lisa, I guess after I discovered that I had bisexual feelings. There's a magazine called *Select*. It's a swingers' magazine. You write in ads about yourself, or you and your wife, and send pictures—sometimes with clothes—mostly without. Then you can write to any couple that attracts you—and get together."

Lisa has been inspecting her nails, and now she looks up. "I know what really started it. That letter I found in the trunk of the car!"

Bill grimaces. "You had to bring that up. I wanted to let that lay. It's dead—just a stupid thing." We look at him expectantly, and he spreads his hands in surrender. "O.K.

I wanted to fool around. I wanted to swing and do all the things I'd fantasized. I had this magazine for a long time before I showed it to Lisa, before we had our talk, so I decided to answer an ad. Don't ask me what I was thinking. Even while I was writing it I said to myself, 'What am I doing?' Finally I crumpled it up. I put it in the trunk of the car and forgot about it. Maybe that was a stupid place to put it. Lisa found it and came upstairs disturbed."

Lisa laughs, a little harshly. "Disturbed is the word."

"I kept bugging her to tell me what's the matter. Well, she finally told me, and I made up a fantastic story, didn't I?"

Lisa says, "Sure, except that I didn't believe it. Come on! You're writing a letter for your friend?"

Bill shrugs. "Except I'm the kind of schmuck that would do something like that. I guess that was what started the argument, and it ended with my saying, 'But you wouldn't understand.'"

"And I asked, 'How can I, if you don't tell me?'"

They're both smiling at each other, and suddenly Bill jumps up. "Hey, you want some more beer? No? How about some coffee?"

I say, "I'd like some," and Bill says, "Hey, Lisa, why don't you make some instant, and get me a glass of water, with ice cubes." He walks around the room and the dog starts up and growls. "Prince! Down!" The dog slinks back, and Bill settles on a chair dragged in from the kitchen. While Lisa puts some water on for the coffee, he says, "That was it. That was when I told Lisa all my sexual hang-ups, all my fantasies. We looked at this *Select* book together, making love, and it brought us closer together because there was a part of me I had always kept apart from her—always—and now this part was out in the open, and there was nothing left to keep us apart, and we were so much closer.

"That night, when I made my confession to her, she said

that if I really wanted to, she would swap with another couple to make me happy." Bill looks up to the kitchen doorway where Lisa is standing, and the two smile at each other, a warm, sharing smile. Bill's eyes are moist. "It really hit me hard that she loves me tremendously, enough to do something she finds repugnant just to make me happy. I said to myself, I'm not gonna ask her to do it. If she loves me that much I'd be a fool. I'd be destroying us even if she'd agree. It would only end up in tragedy for our love. So instead, we'd look at this magazine—looking at these good-looking naked women really turned me on—and we'd make love for two or three hours. Fantastic!"

Lisa brings in the mugs of coffee and settles herself on the couch. Bill sips his water and nods. "Then she found a picture of a woman from New Jersey. The magazine is regional, divided into different parts of the country, and this woman turned Lisa on, and she told me about it. You know, in the book *Tropic of Cancer* by Miller there's a sequence where two women, this guy's wife and the neighbor upstairs, they get together and make love and he joins the two women.

"Now Lisa told me that had excited her, but she never admitted it. It was one of her fantasies. I said, 'Why didn't you tell me before?' but you know, even if she had, I don't think we were emotionally mature enough to have handled it. But that night we talked about it, and we fantasized what we would do if we had this woman in bed with us."

Bill leans forward and his eyes glisten. "I've got a fantastic imagination. I really do—the positions that I dreamed up! Well, this really gave a charge to our sex life. We'd make love for hours. Instead of just having an ejaculation, we'd both have orgasms." He shakes his head at the memory. "Our sex life was always good, but it went from good to fantastic."

With just a touch of reproving smugness, Lisa says, "No, it went from *great* to fantastic."

"From great to fantastic," Bill corrects himself. "You can count on one hand how many times we have not had a mutual orgasm after twelve years of being together." And he looks at Lisa with tenderness. "I never really appreciated what I had, but I do now." His voice suddenly becomes serious, each word weighted. "I do just as much as I can to see that my wife gets everything she deserves, which is everything on God's green earth—what she's done for me!"

There is a long, almost reverent silence, and finally I break it to ask, "When did you do something about getting together with another woman?"

"Before we did anything, we talked about it." He throws up his hands. "God, how we talked, and it got to the point—discussing a threesome with another woman—where it was an obsession. We'd go out driving around the Village, the West Side—we wanted to pick somebody up."

"You sound as if you only thought of it in terms of another woman," I ask. "What about another man?"

Very quickly, Bill cuts in. "I couldn't handle another man making love to my wife." Then, as if to soften it, "She doesn't want me really making love to another woman." At my puzzled look, he explains. "It wouldn't be actual sexual intercourse. It would just be touching, Frenching, kissing—that type of thing."

"And when did you finally do something?"

Bill begins to explain. "We had a neighbor we knew was gay. She had told Lisa about this—well, she's a good friend of ours even though we don't feel that much friends with her anymore because she's such a damned drag. You'll be in a good mood, and she'll come along and dump all her troubles on you. Who needs that? Anyway, I kept bugging Lisa to call her up. I'd say, 'Call Rhonda. Call her up and tell her you're interested.'"

Lisa laughs with a touch of triumph. "But I didn't tell her.

I asked her up when Bill was home, and I made *him* tell her everything."

Bill shakes his head disgustedly. "Typical Rhonda. She takes it to mean my wife is turning gay and wants another woman, and she starts telling me I should just sit there and watch. At first I thought she was talking about her gay girl friends, but then I realize she means herself! And she's a married woman. She's got two kids."

"But you set it up with her?"

"We had to make arrangements. Her husband goes bowling on Tuesday, and that's the night I have this training course in TV repair, so I had to get out of it. After her husband went bowling, the plan was Lisa would go down to her apartment and the two of them would get involved and then she'd call me and I'd come down and watch them, then join in.

"A half hour passed and the phone didn't ring, and I began to wonder what the hell was going on. Then the call came, and I asked, 'Well?' and Lisa says they're too nervous, too uncomfortable. They were drinking blackberry brandy to try and relax. I was pretty excited by then, so I went down there and joined them. I took a copy of *Screw* magazine along, you know, to break the ice, and after a while Lisa began to loosen up."

Bill smiles, remembering, and he reaches over and takes Lisa's hand. "The three of us were sitting on the couch down there, Rhonda with her hand under Lisa's arm, massaging her left breast while I was on the other side, reading from the magazine. Then I saw Rhonda lean over and kiss her and she whispered, 'Do you wanna go in the other room?'

"They went in and lay down on the bed, and she started to suck on Lisa's breast, and put her hand in her pants, you know, but instead of reacting with her usual passion, Lisa just lay there like a piece of meat loaf."

Lisa grimaces. "And that's just what I felt like!"

Bill chuckles. "She didn't look like she was getting any big kick out of it, so I helped Rhonda take her pants off, then Rhonda started to French her, and I could see something was wrong."

Lisa nods. "Something was."

"I asked her if there was something she wanted me to do, and she says, 'Yes, lick my legs!' so I started tonguing her legs, and then I got involved and took my pants off and joined in, and there we were, the two of them making love to each other, and I was making love to my wife, and then I was having intercourse from behind with my wife, doggie style, and my wife was eating Rhonda—but you know, Rhonda was just kind of lying there, groaning and moaning, not really getting into it.

"We're different, Lisa and me. We're pretty wild in bed. We really go at it. We really have a good time. If we're going to have a threesome, well, we want that same kind of reaction. We want to take as well as give. This was kind of disappointing. I mean, Rhonda is the butch type, masculine and kind of threatening, and she didn't really turn me on. I didn't enjoy kissing her." Bill laughs. "Enjoy? The next day at work I was fixing a set and suddenly I remembered, and I turned my head and spit, pooh, pooh. The guy next to me says, 'What the hell's the matter with you?' I tell him I was just thinking about the chick I kissed last night, and he says, 'Wow! If that's your reaction, why the hell did you kiss her?'

"I don't know why I kissed her."

Laughing, Lisa says, "I know."

Bill makes a half-affectionate, half-threatening gesture. "We didn't drag it out. Lisa had an orgasm with me, and then she brought Rhonda off. Rhonda was so high she was floating—really smashed. Before we left she hugged Lisa and asked, 'Did you enjoy it? Did you really enjoy it?' It got me mad, like she was trying to take my wife away, like a man might. If I said anything I would have told her off, so I kept my mouth shut, but she grabs my hand when I'm leaving and says, 'You're a really with-it guy, but I would have liked to have Lisa alone for the first time!' "

Bill purses his lips at the memory. "What does she think? My wife wants to become a lesbian? That's not true. We want to share. My wife and I wanted to share her."

"Did you get together with her again?" I ask.

"Yeah. We did it once more with her. We gave her another chance. It wasn't bad. We got the kids out and made love up here, but she wouldn't let me into her. She said, with a woman she doesn't feel like she's cheating on her husband. But that's just her psychological cop-out. If she goes to bed with anyone, man or woman, she's cheating. Who the hell is she trying to kid?

"I came home for lunch a few weeks later when Lisa was in the kitchen and Rhonda was up here, and I tried to get the threesome going again. We got into the bedroom, and Lisa and I were kissing, and Rhonda went down between Lisa's legs and I said I wanted to get on top of her, but she gets indignant. 'What did I tell you about that?' What nerve! I felt like saying, 'Get your hands off my wife and get out of here!' Luckily, one of her kids started to cry—they were playing outside, and that broke it up. Rhonda had to leave. I shut the door and said, 'To hell with her!' and went back to the business of making love to my wife, like a husband should . . . wild and fantastic . . . even though it had to be a quickie because it was my lunch hour."

Lisa asks, "Would you like some more coffee?" When I shake my head, she says, "How about crackers? I have some nice cheese." In spite of my protests, she brings in a plate of cheese and crackers. I stretch and the dog growls menacingly, and Bill says, "Down Prince! Get back to your corner!"

I ask Lisa, "How did you feel about Rhonda?"

Biting her fingernail, she frowns, "I was very confused."

Very quickly, Bill adds, "She was just coming out. It was new awakening for her, the fact that she was bisexual."

"Was Rhonda the first woman you had ever been with, or were there others?"

Thoughtfully, Lisa says, "I fooled with my girl friend when we were kids. We were only eleven—I guess all kids do. No, I don't really consider that anything. Rhonda was really my first—as a grownup."

"And it wasn't what we expected," Bill adds. "We expected something fantastic—wild!"

"What did you do after that?"

"Well—" Bill considered. "We'd seen ads in the *Village Voice* for bisexual women, and we thought we'd go there, to the Village, and meet one. Once we went out to look for this gay bar, to find a woman for the two of us. Since then I've found out there's no such thing as—well, it's impossible to find a woman. We tried Brothers and Sisters, a bar on Forty-sixth Street, but I was all filled with guilt."

"Why?"

"Well, it was like I was using my wife as bait, which kind of caused a guilt complex. Anyway, when we went there it was all men. We took a table all the way in the back, but there was a guy near us who kept looking at me. I felt very self-conscious."

Lisa laughs, a bit cruelly, and Bill protests. "No, listen, I always dreamed about that, being sought after and all, but when it actually happened—well, like every fantasy, it's not so good when you live it."

"Now you know how women feel," Lisa murmurs.

"Sure, but when I look at a woman, if she's not interested she keeps walking. Hey, I've had my opportunities, and I always will. There's a certain segment of women who find a guy with a great personality—like I have—who's moderately good-looking; they find him attractive, which some women have found me."

Lisa laughs. "I keep remembering how that guy looked at you."

"Yeah. Well, that bar was all gay. There was a guy behind each guy at the bar, talking to him. One guy who was sitting at the bar turned around, and the guy behind him kissed him full on the lips. Wow!"

"Did you go to any other gay bars?"

"No. We were really disappointed. But I kept pushing and looking. I was determined to make it happen. But Lisa felt we should let it happen by itself, and then it would be beautiful." He smiles at her. "She's so right."

"What did you do after that?"

"Mostly we went to Bi-Lib meetings, and there were never any females. My wife was the only woman."

"Bi-Lib?"

"Bisexual Liberation. They advertise in the *Village Voice*. We had good rap sessions there, and I found that it helped me as a person to talk about my faults, my need to prove my toughness and all of that. Talking about that really helped me."

"But you went there looking for a woman?"

Bill nods. "Yeah, but I also found it very, very warm. After the first five minutes I felt as if I had stopped searching for sex, and I started feeling like everyone there cared about me as a human being. They cared about my human emotions and wanted to be with me on a human level."

Lisa nods as Bill explains this. "There was one young man there who said, after you get through the tricking stage, you want to meet people, not bodies. I remember that."

"And that's where it's all at right now," Bill adds.

"Have you met another person?" I ask. "Someone who can give you the kind of relationship you want?"

Bill looks at Lisa. "There was Marty and Sue."

Cutting a wedge of cheese, she says, "I met Anne first."

"Oh, yeah, Anne. Lisa was introduced to Anne over the

phone by someone from the Bi-Lib group, and she came over to visit. They liked each other."

With a little smile Lisa corrects him. "It was a lot more than like."

"I guess it was. They made love on the couch, and I find that very erotic."

"Were you there?" I ask.

"No." Chewing his lip, Bill shakes his head. "Not that I wouldn't have loved to, but it wasn't possible. Anne's married and has two kids, and right now she's trying to pull her life together."

"Did you mind Lisa being alone with her?"

"At first I minded it like hell. After I heard they made love, I was angry at her because she was having all the fun and I was out in the cold. I felt rejected, like she was saying your wife is great, but fuck you!"

"How did Lisa feel about her?"

"Lisa has this philosophy that before she can go to bed with a woman she has to get to know her. My wife doesn't want only sex. She wants a relationship."

Lisa nods. "I don't want a one-night stand. It was something else with Anne."

"I talked to Anne a couple of times on the phone, and she's really a warm, kind person," Bill explains. "I tried to set up a threesome, but she didn't want to. So then I thought maybe I could watch the two of them, but she wouldn't go along with that. She said she'd feel too self-conscious. I started to get really angry, but then I thought, what the hell, I've got a lot of balls. Here's a married woman with her own problems, trying to save her marriage, and I'm trying to get her into a situation with a total stranger. I did a lot of thinking then, and finally I told Lisa, 'If you want to get together with Anne and make love, beautiful.'"

"What did you say, Lisa?"

Smiling, Lisa says, "I told him I'd turn the tape recorder

on in the bedroom and he could hear what's going on." She shrugged. "Well, he's always asking me, what went on? What did you say? That turns him on."

"Did you mind the recorder?"

"No. I liked it. It made me feel that Bill was sharing Anne with me, even though he wasn't there."

"I tell her positions to try, things to do. When Lisa and I are making love, I say, 'Try this with Anne. Do this with her, do that.' When they get together a part of me is with them, because it's me that thought all those positions up."

"And do you feel any jealousy about them?"

Emphatically, Bill says, "Not at all. What I do feel, I feel guilty that I once felt jealous. I feel guilty that I ever felt resentment to Lisa. What the hell, I started the whole thing. She didn't."

"Have you ever had any experience with other men since this started?"

Very quickly, Bill says, "No! I really have no desire to. There was a period when I was attracted to men, the successful, mature businessman type. A distinguished gentleman. I guess partly I wanted the affection of an older man, and partly I wanted to be with someone I respected."

"So since Lisa discovered her bisexuality, you've given up yours."

"Well—" Bill considers. "We once got into a foursome, that was with Sue and Marty. We met them at a Bi-Lib social. She was a college student." There's a touch of reverence in Bill's voice. "Marty, he was just a mixed-up guy. Not really a bisexual. I think he went along with it just because of Sue."

"Sue was really something special," Lisa says with a little smile.

Bill chuckles. "She was. They had to leave the social at ten-thirty. It was in Manhattan and they had to get to Brooklyn. They said it would take an hour and a half by subway, so I offered to drive them."

"Did anything happen that night?" I ask.

"We got to know each other. We stopped at McDonald's and had cheeseburgers, and we sat around and talked, and while we're sitting there I say to Sue, 'I'd like to have a foursome with you,' and she says, 'All right.' Just like that. But that's all I said. I brought it up. She accepted, and that was it. You don't bet on something like that."

"When did you get together?"

"We made plans for the next Sunday. We invited them to the house for a turkey dinner. I picked them up in Manhattan and bought some cheese and chopped liver at the kosher deli, and it was just a nice day. It really was." He sighs. "You put four nice people together who have common interests and who genuinely like each other, and that's it."

"What did you do?"

"We sat right here, didn't we, Lisa?"

Lisa nods, and Bill goes on. "We had chopped liver and wine and Cheddar cheese, and that Danish butternut cheese —and creamed herring, too. I love creamed herring. Afterward Lisa was in the kitchen fixing the turkey and I brought in the dishes, and she said, 'I think they want to go to bed.' I said, 'Oh, wow, I didn't realize that!' So I came inside and told them, 'Hey, why don't you two go into the bedroom?' and at first Marty was kind of shy and self-conscious, but I said, 'Look, if you want to, go ahead. You know, nobody's gonna bother you. Go in and enjoy.' So they enjoyed."

"You didn't join them?"

He spreads his hands. "We had to get dinner ready, and anyway, the first time it helped them unwind. I had bought a scented candle, and I put it in the bedroom—Sue's really into scents. They really appreciated that. You know, it makes me feel good to do nice things for people. I like to make people happy, know what I mean? I like to be a nice guy."

We smile at each other, and Bill shakes his head, remembering. "When they came out they had that nice feeling, like after you make love, you know? They had that high. Then we had our turkey dinner, and it was good, wasn't it, Honey?"

Lisa's voice is so soft I can hardly hear her. "Delicious."

Bill says, "Hey! Are you thinking about something else?"

Defensively, Lisa says, "No. I said it was delicious."

Bill spreads his hands. "So I'm doing all the talking."

"Well, you usually do."

Bill laughs and turns to me. "She lets me talk until I say something wrong. Then she cuts me down to size."

With some satisfaction, Lisa says, "That's exactly right."

I steer Bill back to his story. "What happened after dinner?"

"We put the kids in their bedroom to play, and we got out these magazines, *Select* and one called *Young Lesbians* and another, and we were looking at them, and Lisa was sitting next to me and Sue next to her on the other side, then Marty. I started feeling my wife's breasts, and we began to get turned on. And then the kids came running out, and we had to shove the magazines out of sight. They go back, and we take them out again. I begin to play with Lisa and Marty with Sue, and then, bang! The kids are in again, and the stuff goes out of sight. Well, after about a half hour of this, Sue says, 'Why don't we go into the bedroom?'

"Great. Like one unit we all got up, took the magazines, and marched into the bedroom."

I ask, "What did you do with the kids?"

"They were in their room, and the door was closed. I locked our bedroom door. We lay on the bed looking at the magazines, and I started fondling Lisa and Marty started on his chick, and you could hear the snaps on her dungarees going, one by one, snap, snap. Then Sue says, 'Why don't we take off our clothes?'

"We all jumped up. It's funny, I've always been self-conscious about my stomach. I never go to the beach because

I'm too fat, yet here I was with a couple we only met once—
our second time together—and we're stripping down."

He shakes his head, remembering. "They were at one end
of the bed, and we were at the other. We both start making
out, me and my wife, and he and his chick, and we're really
having a good time."

The dog comes out of his corner and whines, and Bill puts
his hand up warningly. "He wants to go out. Not now, Prince.
Honey, give him some water. Please?"

Lisa takes care of the dog and Bill says, "It's a funny
thing. Marty had never done the sixty-nine before, and Lisa
and me, we're very masterful at it. And he was watching us,
and I felt self-conscious." Bill shakes his head. "I had trouble
keeping an erection. So finally I said, 'Why don't you join
us?' and first Sue looked surprised, then she said, 'Oh, wow!
Yeah, all right.' And she came over and started running
her fingers over our bodies, and I just looked at her. I wanted
to kiss her—she had such an unbelievably lovely body, dainty
—and she leaned over and smiled and gave me a French
kiss. My God, I never felt such a tongue!"

Bill shakes his head at the memory. "It got pretty wild.
At one point I was on Lisa's breast and Sue was on her other,
and Lisa was on one of Sue's breasts and Sue's other breast
was empty! So I look at Marty and say, 'Why don't you join
in? There's one tit doing nothing.'" Bill laughs and his
stomach shakes. "Marty joined us—quick!"

"We stopped after a few minutes, and I said to Marty and
Sue, 'Why don't you two try the sixty-nine?' and Marty says,
'We never have,' so I do it to show him, and pretty soon she
began to have, like, spasms, and Marty gets scared and yells,
'Sue! Sue! What's happening? Are you having a heart attack?'

"Well, I tell you, we all got hysterical and broke up. It
was that kind of afternoon."

"And Marty?" I ask. "Did you do anything with him?"

Bill looks quickly at Lisa, and then nods. "At one point we

were all in a heap. I had Sue's behind in my face and I was eating her, and someone went down on me, but I could tell it was Lisa—after all these years—and I reached out and felt this penis—you know? I held it and I felt kind of strange. I couldn't see what was going on. I just felt around blindly. I guess I wanted to see his reaction—we were all having a really fantastic time." He hesitates for a moment, chewing his lip as he remembers, and Lisa watches him quietly.

Finally, with a little shake, Bill says, "It was getting kind of late, so we got dressed, and I told my daughter we were going to drive them home and she should watch the kids. She loves baby-sitting 'cause she can stay up late and watch TV.

"So we were driving back to Brooklyn on the Belt Parkway, nine-thirty, ten o'clock on Sunday night, and the traffic was heavy, so we stopped at McDonald's like we did before. But Sue kept worrying about what she'd tell her parents, and I thought that was funny. She had said she was eighteen and in college. What was she worried about? We should have picked up the signs that something was wrong."

Lisa says, "We should have, because she hit us right away about the age difference. She said, 'Age doesn't make any difference, does it?'"

Bill frowns. "Honey, that was as we were walking out."

"No, as we were going in."

"Yeah, you're right. I told her, 'No. We all get along great.'"

Lisa smiles. "Later she hit us with it. She said, 'How would you feel about doing it with a fifteen-year-old?'"

Bill cuts in. "She told us she's really fifteen and Marty's sixteen, just smack in the face like that. My first reaction was God, we're gonna get arrested for corrupting the morals of a minor!"

"What did you do?"

"What could we do? Nothing. We drove them home, but

we still had a wild time on the ride, Sue and Marty playing around in the back and Lisa fooling with me in the front seat. You know, the whole afternoon—the dinner, the creamed herring, the lovemaking in the bedroom and then in the car—it was just a beautiful experience."

"But there was really no feeling between you and Marty?" I ask.

Uncomfortably, Bill says, "No. We were just buddies."

"Do you think," I ask slowly, "that since the whole thing has come out in the open, since there's been this honesty between you and Lisa, there's been no drive toward other men?"

Considering, Bill says slowly, "Yeah. I think so."

Lisa frowns. "I don't know. I wonder—"

"There wasn't much of a drive before because I wasn't really homosexual," Bill says quickly.

"But you talked about the need for love and affection."

"That's right."

"And you don't feel that need anymore?"

"I haven't felt it for a while," Bill frowns. "I had a friend I used to see now and then, and I went to bed with him, but we never got into any real heavy lovemaking. We just kind of fooled around. He loves to get on my back—I'm a well-built guy, even though I'm fat. I've got a good set of muscles. He'd masturbate me, but I'd never have an ejaculation. I'd come home and make love to Lisa."

"Do you still see him?"

Bill hesitates. "I like the guy—I still do. Actually, I've been trying to get in touch with him because I asked Lisa, 'Do you want to see me making it with a guy?' and she says, 'Honestly, I don't know.' I'm not all that wild about it myself, but if it happens with a couple we really dig, and two of us men want to start fooling around with each other— that's all it would be, just fooling around. No emotional involvement, just a grab and, you know, just playing around with each other—it wouldn't be very heavy because I'm not all that interested."

Bill is silent for a while, thoughtful, and finally I ask, "Where do the children fit into this whole thing? Is it a problem or not? When you have another couple over, do you maneuver around the kids?"

Lisa nods. "It can be a problem." More thoughtfully than before, she adds, "A big problem."

Very quickly, Bill cuts in. "Yeah. That's why the ideal woman for us to get to know would be a single woman with her own apartment where we can sit down, get undressed— not necessarily make love right away, but talk, listen to music." He shakes his head. "This is a hassle, the kids walking in and out. Hell, I think we're entitled to our own private sex life. It's not as if we're taking anything away from the kids. We're still devoting ourselves to them as much as we can."

"It's what we are entitled to outside of the children," Lisa adds.

Bill says, "We have to be able to grow as people ourselves."

"And that," Lisa agrees, "is a hard lesson for parents to learn. We're just learning it after eleven years."

Uncertain, I ask, "But how do you feel about it? Bill is right. He talks so much that I don't really know anything about your feelings."

Frowning, Lisa says, "I'm still really, more or less, finding myself out. I enjoy it, but I've only had a few encounters with other women. The one time I was alone with another woman I felt that it was satisfying, but after she left I wanted my husband home."

"Do you feel it's done anything to your relationship?"

Pursing her lips and considering, Lisa says, "It's put Bill together more than it's affected me." Turning to Bill questioningly, she asks, "Isn't that right?"

"Uh-huh. Definitely so."

"You don't feel that it's loosened you up or cooled you?" I ask.

"Yeah. It freed me a bit—left me to explore a little bit." There is a long pause, and almost with a sigh Lisa says, "I don't know. Maybe because I haven't done it that many times—the fantasy is still greater than the real thing."

"Do you have any guilts about it?"

Very firmly, she answers, "No! None whatever." Pushing her hair back, she sits up straighter and adds, "I think it's because we talked it over beforehand, and it wasn't as if we were hiding it from each other. If I had felt the need for another woman and I found someone without Bill knowing about it, I would have felt guilt. But now I don't in the least."

"Well, it was because of me that these feelings were awakened in you," Bill reminds her.

"I'm not saying differently, am I?"

"You really have nothing to feel guilty about because I started the whole business."

Lisa brushes this aside. "Look, when you're a little child and you're exploring sex, you do feel guilty. I used to feel guilty about what I did when I was a child. Why else do you close the door and try to hide things?"

"What was your childhood like?" I ask.

"I guess it was fairly normal." Lisa smiles. "Pretty much happy. I was an only child and used to get my own way. It was pretty easygoing. Most of the time, though, I spent with my grandfather. My mother had to work, and he used to watch me. He was a widower. My father and mother worked together."

"Did you finish high school?"

"Yeah. I got married while I was in high school. Then the kids came. My first daughter wasn't planned. She was an accident."

"No! She wasn't an accident," Bill interrupts.

"I guess not. If you don't use protection, you get caught sooner or later."

"We used it as an excuse to get married," Bill explains. "I wanted to, but I was afraid to take the responsibility. This made me."

"We were going through too many hassles with my mother," Lisa adds. "Bill wasn't Jewish, and when I married him my mother was pretty hysterical, but my father was fairly calm. My mother didn't want me to get married. She said, 'I'll take the baby and raise it like my own.'" Turning to Bill, she says, "I don't know if I ever told you about that."

Surprised, he says, "No. You never told me. Anyway, I converted after we got married, and that made her happy. I don't practice, but our daughter goes to Hebrew school. She's smart, too."

"Did you finish high school?" I ask Bill.

"I dropped out after my father died. That was my junior year and I was kind of lost. My mother was running around a lot. I hung out with a tough crowd." Bill shakes his head as if clearing the memories away. "Now I wish I'd stayed and learned more, maybe I could have learned to make our marriage work earlier."

Quickly, Lisa says, "It's working now."

"Well, our bisexuality has drawn us much closer together as a couple, not just sexually but emotionally. We're more one complete person than two different people. We're like two halves of the same person, and it's not just a desire to share the same woman. Before, there were certain things I'd never do. I'd never help her with the laundry, take her to a laundromat. Now it's a regular thing. Last night I went down by myself and brought up the clothes."

Lisa laughed. "That used to be a no-no."

"I never did that before in eleven years."

"It was too sissyish," Lisa teases.

Earnestly, Bill says, "Now we do laundry on Sundays. We hold hands and walk into the candy store and buy magazines. We do our shopping together. It's just brought us so close. Look, when you can share something as intimate as bisexuality and without any apprehensions, what's left to hold you apart?

"Look, I just firmly believe I couldn't find another woman —I don't want another woman, because I love my wife very deeply and sincerely, and I don't want to change my life with her. I want to grow with her and mature with her and be a better provider."

"If you had your choice," I ask later, when I'm getting ready to leave, "would you want a relationship with one other woman, or with a couple like Marty and Sue?"

Promptly, Bill says, "One woman."

"And you, Lisa?"

"I think so."

"Is it because you see a man as a threat to the two of you?"

"Kind of, yeah . . ." Bill says thoughtfully. "We have this mutual understanding. We talk out everything fully. Lisa says she doesn't want me scoring another woman, and she knows I don't want another man scoring her. I guess it boils down to what's good for the goose is good for the gander." He hesitates. "Still, if the three of us were in bed in one of our positions, like all involved with each other, and I started screwing the other chick—she wouldn't find that objectionable. But if I were to grab her and start balling her, then she'd get pissed off and want to castrate me, you know, right there on the spot. She told me, 'You want to put it there so bad, you leave it there.'"

When I leave, after making a fuss over the dog, I walk the few blocks to my car. It's a pleasant night and the houses look less shabby in the glow of the street light. Here and there people have taken lawn chairs outside and are sitting in groups talking. I wonder if Rhonda is one of them.

Near my car a group of teen-agers are playing cards, but they move aside politely as I come up. There's no sense of the city here. Maybe it's a nice place to raise children.

At first glance the word "bisexual" appears to be self-explanatory: a bisexual person is one who has engaged in sexual acts with both sexes. It is not as simple as it might appear.

If a person has had one or two bisexual experiences, can we say that person is a "bisexual"? What if these bisexual experiences were engaged in many years ago? Would that qualify one to be classified as a bisexual? If a person is strictly heterosexual, but from time to time has erotic sexual thoughts about the same sex, does that make one a bisexual? Many men have felt the desire to throw their arms around another man and perhaps even kiss him. In our present American culture few men like to admit such thoughts and feelings, but they are there. Would simply having thoughts like these classify one as a bisexual? Many people think so, on the assumption that unless something was going on underneath the thoughts would not be there. They accept the old saying, "Where there's smoke, there's fire."

To be a bisexual, I believe at least two things are necessary: (1) a repeated pattern of overt sexual acts with both sexes; and (2) an active enjoyment of both sexes during the sexual acts. Thus, a bisexual is a person who engages in and enjoys sexual acts with members of both sexes.

Are Bill and Lisa really bisexual, as they claim? Lisa has been the bisexual partner while Bill has remained in his heterosexual role. It was Lisa who first verbalized her attraction to the body of one of the women pictured in the swingers' magazine *Select.* It was Lisa who made the contact with the neighbor next door. Up to this point she included Bill, but when she met Anne it was only the two of them who had sex. There seems little question that Lisa enjoys the lesbian part of bisexuality. When Bill said, "Anne and she liked each other," Lisa quickly added, "It was a lot more than like!" Even though Lisa entered into bisexual activity at the urging of Bill, and states she is "still confused" about the entire development, it's quite evident that she can enjoy sex with either male or female partners with little or no guilt feelings.

Lisa does little talking, but when she does, Bill listens. One gets the distinct impression that she is the strong member in the marriage. She is secure enough in her position to let him take over the conversation and satisfy his need to be the man of the house. There was no hostility on her part toward him, although one might expect some in view of his inability to cope with his psychological problems. During the years Bill was losing one job after another because of his emotional problems, Lisa had a difficult time making things work out between the two of them. When Bill came home and accused her of having sex with another man, he would find her washing the dishes or doing the laundry. These types of emotional problems brought about by conflicts within Bill's head could easily have led Lisa to be quite angry and express this anger in aggression and hostility. It was obvious she was in love with Bill and enjoyed her role as the stable influence in the home.

Lisa said their sex life during the entire marriage was great. Bill was emphatic about it also. Bill mentioned he couldn't remember more than five occasions during their twelve years of marriage when they did not have an orgasm at the same time. Even taking Bill's statement with a few grains of salt, we would have to conclude that he regards his sexual life with his wife as highly satisfactory. In light of this history we could not say that bisexuality was begun in order to revive a faltering marital sex life. There are people in the "swingers" set who engage in wife swapping in order to make their lousy sex life come alive again. This was certainly not the case with Bill and Lisa. Sexually, she had no complaint either before or after the bisexual experience. When Bill said their sex life went from "good to fantastic," Lisa quickly corrected him, adding, "No, it went from *great* to fantastic."

I would say Lisa is rapidly adjusting to a bisexual life, and as long as her husband feels the need to have this dimension added to his marriage, she will continue. On the other hand, if he were to want it stopped, she would go along with that also. Bisexual experiences were not sought out by Lisa, and her main objective seems to be the emotional health of her husband. If it's good for Bill, she will continue bisexual experiences; if it's not good for him, she will stop.

Bill has been quite insecure for a number of years, and the accumulation of these insecurities once led to a crisis state serious enough to require hospitalization for a short time. He lost his father and could not count on his mother. His fantasies involved finding a wealthy older Jewish woman on whom he could rely. His relationship with his father was one in which he was told what to do and he did it. He felt he never got any real attention or love from either parent. When he was older he got into one scrape after another, usually trying to uphold his image as a man. He also went into amateur boxing. His work record is one of a succession of jobs that he lost partially because of his belligerent attitudes and actions. He feels it is unmasculine to cry.

His emotional floundering lasted for well over five years, until he found his strength was right in his own home, in the form of his wife. When Bill "confessed" his sexual fantasy life to his wife—when he told her about his actual homosexual experiences—he was telling her the things he felt were the weakest parts of himself. These were the thoughts and actions that were the ultimate in not being a man. He was certain he would be rejected by her. He had not counted on the strength of his wife and her understanding that he might need to live out his fantasy life in order to keep himself "together."

Bill's homosexual experiences were always with an older man, in which he played the passive role. Psychiatric help has aided him in understanding that he was looking for the strength of an older man as a substitute for his father. It was true that his father had strength, but he didn't convey any warmth to Bill, who found this warmth and acceptance through his homosexual encounters. At the present time, it would be difficult to classify Bill as a bisexual if we stick to our definition of a bisexual as one who has sex with either sex and enjoys it. Bill does not now have sex with men, and says he really isn't interested in it. At the same time, he has asked his wife if she would like to see him have sexual relations with a man. If she expresses any desire to see this, there is little doubt in my mind that Bill would comply and have a bisexual experience. However, it is doubtful if he would enjoy it, because the need to find warmth and sympathetic strength has been fulfilled by his wife.

What have these experiences done to their marriage? Both stated strongly that their bisexual experiences brought them closer together than they ever thought possible. From the words they used and from total nonverbal communication between them, there was no question that they were very close emotionally. There was no hostility, no one-upmanship, no undercutting. There was a complete display of deep warmth, affection, and true tenderness. One's heart and feelings went out to both of them for their depth of sincerity and honesty. On the other hand, I don't think it is the sexual aspect of bisexuality that has affected their marriage, but something quite different. It seems to me that when Bill found that what he thought was weakness in himself was totally accepted by his wife, he could then relax and not need to fight the world. All the warm and tender feelings hidden by him through a veil of aggression and hostility could now become operational. This honest exchange of his deepest fears led him to know that he could share anything with the woman he loved, and this in turn deepened their love for each other. It was not the bisexual experiences that brought them together; it was the honest expression of deep-seated fears and their acceptance of these fears and of each other that brought their marriage together.

3
Clark

I meet Clark in the coffee shop of his hotel on Lexington Avenue in the Fifties. He's a big man, in his late forties, with a handsome face and close-cut white hair. He's heavy, but his size lets him carry his extra weight well. He could pass for the Hollywood conception of a banker or businessman. We order coffee and size each other up.

"I'm not at all sure that I want to get involved in this."

"I won't urge you, but if you're concerned about security . . ."

"It's not that," he interrupts. "My wife knows about me."

"You mean she's found out since you've been married?"

"Oh, no. I told her before we were married. I've always swung both ways."

"How did she take it?"

He shrugs. "Well, she married me. The only thing she asked was that I shouldn't rub her nose in it. She doesn't ever want to know what I do, nor does she want my sons to find out, and that's fair enough."

"Do you agree with your wife that the kids shouldn't know?"

"Hell, yes." He hesitates, frowning a bit. "Not that I think there's anything wrong with it. But it would only confuse them. They're just ten and twelve, and they're not old enough to know what sex is all about."

"If they knew, do you think they'd hate you?"

Looking down, he rubs the knuckles of one hand with the other. "I don't know. Kids are funny. I'm sure it would confuse them, but you never know nowadays."

"But how do you feel about it?"

"Personally, I don't think it makes me any less a man because I have sex with another man, but I can see how, in their young minds, it might."

"Do you think it could push them toward homosexuality?"

"No."

"Would it upset you if they were homosexual or bisexual when they grew up?"

"I wouldn't be too happy about it. They'd have a much easier life if they grew up heterosexual. I know it's caused me plenty of problems. I'd just hate the kids to have to face stuff like that."

"Does your wife feel the same way?"

"I guess she feels that a regular man doesn't need that kind of outlet, and my kids would look down on me if they found out."

He stirs some sugar into his coffee and frowns at the cup. "You like ice cream in your coffee?"

"Sure."

He signals the waitress and orders a dish of vanilla ice cream.

"If she feels like that, how do you live a bisexual life?"

"I work for a drug house and I travel a lot, like this trip. I have a room at the hotel, and I'll be here a week. I'll get my fill of men, and that'll hold me when I get back home."

"I'm not sure I know what you mean by your fill of men."

He smiles. "I'm not sure myself. As many as I need, I guess."

"Has that ever happened?"

He hesitates. "Not really. My strength gives out." He laughs. "If I could, I'd have a man every hour on the hour."

"You don't fool around at home?"

"Look, I live in a small town in Alabama. I can't take a crap there without every neighbor knowing about it. I keep my nose clean at home. It's a typical Southern town. There are about forty thousand people, but we live out in the suburbs. Everyone knows everyone else's business, at least at my income level. We have a nice split-level, and I take care of it myself, cut the grass every weekend, do the usual chores around the house. We're pretty friendly with our neighbors—parties, bridge, the usual visiting back and forth. Nothing much goes on there. Even in the local newspaper the big excitement is local politics—there's hardly anything about Watergate. It's all the bond issue or the local school, that sort of thing. I guess we're pretty provincial."

"But you like it?"

He sits back and folds his arms. "Let's say it's important to me that my neighbors think a lot of me. I take pride in that. You know, it's important for the kids to have their father respected in the community. That's why I don't fool around at home. Hell, if I was ever caught, I'd be ridden out of town on a rail!"

"Are you afraid of that?"

He nods. "You better believe I'm afraid. I'm scared shitless that someone will recognize me and blow the whistle on me. My wife would just die if this came out. Not just for the kids, but our friends, too. Can you imagine what they'd say if they knew her husband went to bed with men? That's why I have my sex life far enough away to be safe."

"It's that bad, huh?"

"Besides, I'd be out on my ass if the company ever suspected. They make it a point to take an interest in their executives' private lives. I have no illusions how fast I'd be fired." He flicks his fingers. "Like that!"

"So you have to be really careful."

"I do. I never tell a guy I pick up my real name or where I come from—and that bothers me."

"How do you mean?"

"Well, I'd like to be direct and honest with the men I meet."

"How do you find men when you travel?"

He looks at me with a smile. "An hour before you came I went down to the hotel's men's room and picked up a guy. I had him in and out of my room in twenty minutes. Christ, if I had the stamina I could get a guy every hour in a city like this."

"How about other cities?"

He shrugs. "Chicago is easy, so is San Francisco. But hell, every city has its places. At least one hotel has a bar, even if it's not a gay bar, where you can pick men up. Or men's rooms. They're the simplest."

His ice cream comes, and he empties half of it into the coffee. "This would be great with a shot of brandy. My wife makes a sensational coffee with brandy and ice cream." He pats his belly. "But I'm laying off. I promised her I'd lose twenty pounds."

"Why did you promise her that?"

"She's always bugging me about being overweight." He smooths out his jacket over his stomach. "I don't think I'm all that much overweight. Well, maybe a bit. But I just want her off my back." His voice sharpens a bit, then relaxes. I'm not saying she's a nag, but she goes on about my weight a lot."

"Is there anything else about you she'd like to change?"

"Well—" he hesitates. "Sure, there's a lot she'd like to see different, leaving the sex thing aside. If I can leave it aside. Actually, she'd rather I wasn't bisexual because, though we don't mention it, I know she's constantly afraid something is going to explode. We talked about it once, and she told me it was like living on a field of land mines, always expecting a blowup."

"Do you think that's why she nags?"

"I don't know. It's more than that. She's annoyed because I don't do enough around the house. I don't take charge of things."

"What does she mean by taking charge?"

He shrugs in annoyance. "I don't know what she means. I don't think I'm any different from the average guy. I cut the grass. O.K., I don't like to do the dishes or help with the wash—I really don't think that's a man's job.

"Don't get me wrong. She's not a 'women's libber,' but she would like me to do more around the house. She doesn't talk about my bisexuality, but she makes little cracks like, 'At least you can be a man around the house.' That makes me mad, because I don't see why I'm any less of a man if I don't do the household chores."

"But why does she want you to lose the weight?"

He stirs the coffee for a moment. "Well, she says I'd be much better in bed. Another crack of hers is, she doesn't see how anyone can make love to fat men. I really resent that, being called fat."

Moving away from this subject, I say, "You talked about the ease of getting sex in a big city. Doesn't that sort of sex disturb you?"

He looks at me over the coffee cup and smiles. "Sex anywhere doesn't disturb me. You know, I don't have to go into men's rooms for it. My business is setting up exhibits for medical conventions, and I have to attend a lot of them. I tell you, you wouldn't believe how many men are willing to fool around, straight men, too—or at least they think they're straight."

"Do you think this is some kind of trend, something new? Or have you always found it this way?"

"I think it's a lot more widespread than the average person realizes. When I was younger, I thought I was different, but now I realize I can find it anyplace. I think eventually it's going to be more common than it is now. It may be the new way of living for people."

"Bisexuality?"

"Well, I think I'm different from the ordinary guy in this situation. I love my wife and I'm happy at home. I have a good sex life with her. But that's not true for most of the men I run into. They're married to someone who won't go to bed with them, and if they do, they don't enjoy sex anyway. That's not my case at all." He hesitates, considering his coffee cup.

I ask him, "How did you explain your bisexual activity to your wife in the beginning?"

"I was honest. I told her it was a need I couldn't control and it was better if I took this outlet instead of adultery. Another man couldn't threaten our marriage in any way, while another woman certainly could."

"How did she react?"

"Oh, she bought it pretty well. Of course, she'd rather it didn't happen. I guess it's hard for her to 'not think' about my having sex with a man. That's why she doesn't want to hear about it."

"You told her you had a need. Do you make any distinction between needing and wanting?"

"Well, it's hard for me to tell the difference between the

two. All I can say is that I don't see how I can stop it." He chews his lip a moment. "To tell you the truth, I don't want to stop it because I think it's a good way to keep my family together. I've got a hell of a sexual drive, and when I'm out of town it's easier to pick up men instead of women."

"You've never had any permanent relationship with a man?"

He sips his coffee thoughtfully. "You know, that's hell on a guy. I mean, getting involved with a married man. I once had a guy who was my lover for over a year, but it's like that book, you know, *Back Street*. We couldn't have any life together."

"Did it create any problems at home?"

"None between my wife and me, because she didn't know anything about it. But it meant a hell of a lot of lying and sneaking around. It was on the same level as having an affair with a woman." He thinks for a moment, then says, "To be perfectly honest, we had more fights and disagreements during that year than we ever did. I guess, in a way, I was really torn."

"How? Was it easy to divide your feelings between the two?"

"Easy? You've got to be kidding. It was hell." He shakes his head. "I have to admit I was in love with both of them for different reasons. I liked the closeness of the man more than the closeness of my wife. It's as if they served two different functions. Enid, my wife, was warm and affectionate, and we had good sex together. It was a different emotional feeling when I was with this guy. I liked to be held by him, to be close to him—it was just a different feeling altogether."

"But she never knew?"

"I never let her know in any way."

"Why not, if she knows you're bisexual?"

"She'd have been too hurt. I'd do anything in the world

to keep from hurting her." He puts his cup down and stares at it for a moment, then he looks up at me intently. "I really love my wife."

"If your wife thought your bisexual life was endangering the family, what would you do?"

"I've thought of that from time to time, and I'm not sure I could make the choice."

"What if you had to?"

After a thoughtful pause, he says, "I'd have to give up bisexuality. There's nothing in the world that's going to make me give up my kids and my wife."

"You've never wanted a homosexual life?"

He shrugs. "I'm not homosexual—at least I think I'm not—but who the hell can put labels on these things? I like men. O.K., I can't do without them, but I can't do without women either. I never could. I started screwing around when I was ten, with older women, the maids, later my mother's friends, the kids at school. I began fooling around with boys at the same time."

"Did it ever bother you?"

"Christ, yes! When I was a kid I thought I was every kind of a pervert. But what the hell, the drive was too much. I'd take a girl out and screw her and take her home, then drive downtown looking for a guy, and on top of it all, I'd get home and masturbate."

"You say when you were a kid you thought of yourself as a pervert. Do you think bisexuality is perverse?"

"No, not at all—but I think it causes some complications."

"Does your wife think it's a perversion?"

"Oh, yes. There's no question about that. She puts up with it because she loves me. But I'm sure she thinks it's perverted."

"Do you still feel guilty about it?"

"Not any more. Somewhere along the line I accepted the

whole thing. That's the way I am, and in a sense I've got the best of both worlds."

"But you're very concerned about these worlds mixing. I'm not quite sure I understand that."

He signals the waitress for another cup of coffee, and when it comes he says, "As long as I'm careful, I'm safe, right? Look, I can take everything I want from the homosexual world, and the best of the heterosexual world, too. It's a good way to live if you don't get caught." He sits back with a smile. "More people ought to try it."

"If you feel that way, why don't you want your kids involved in it?"

"If they grew up and made it their choice when they were older, it would be different. But kids are very susceptible to environment. They may not be able to make up their own minds, and I feel that everyone should make up his own mind about this. You make your own choices, and no one should tell you what to do. That's why I'm glad my wife didn't try and talk me out of my bisexuality."

"Are you active or passive in your homosexual roles?"

He laughs. "I'm whatever the role demands."

"What do you mean?"

"Look, ninety per cent of these things are games. I'll meet a guy and he's a slave."

"A what?"

"A slave. He wants me to slap him around. I've had real rough types pick me up and force me to do that to them. I enjoy that, too. That's the name of the game. You play roles. We all know it's play, but it's fun."

"Do you play roles with women, too?"

He looks faintly shocked. "I don't fool around with women. I'm a very monogamous guy. I'd feel I was betraying my wife if I slept with another woman."

"Isn't sleeping with men an act of sexual betrayal?"

"No. I think it has to do with the question of affection and love. If you say you're in love with a man, it's a different kind of thing from being in love with your wife. There are no promises that you'll marry the man, have children with him. Look, it's pretty superficial to start with. It's only sex. You get home to your wife and you have your family, your children, a whole other thing."

"Have you ever been caught?"

"God, yes. Twice!"

"What happened?"

"When we lived in Ohio and the boys were just babies, there was—well, kind of an incident. Some teen-ager claimed I molested him."

"Did you?"

"Hell, no! My wife stuck with me, but the fact that she knew about me—I don't know what she believed. Things were rough, and my lawyer advised me not to fight it. We just picked up and left town. Funny thing is, the same kid accused another man a month later, and he went to court and it turns out the kid had been doing it right along, oh, maybe ten times, and his parents believed him each time." He chews his lip a moment. "I'm not sure, though, that if it happened now I would run away. Maybe I wasn't being a man about it. I think a real man would stand up and fight for his innocence."

"What was the other incident?"

He waves his hand disgustedly. "I deserved that. I broke my own rule and took up with a neighbor. He was married, too, and I thought we'd be safe, but he decided to divorce his wife and live with me, even though I said, 'Nothing doing.' He made a big stink with both our wives. His wife left him. Enid stuck with me." He shakes his head wonderingly. "She's really a terrific gal—more than I deserve. I don't think I could live without her."

"Why not?"

"My whole life is built around my family."

"But how is she more than you deserve?"

"Well, she stuck with me when things were rough, when that kid made a stink, when we were having a tough financial time afterward—not many women would be that loyal."

"But shouldn't every wife be like that?"

He looks up, his eyes narrowed. "You bet your life they should. But how many are? Look, in marriage you have to count on each other, protect each other. It's like that with my kids, too. If anyone hits them or pushes them around, they have me to contend with. And I've taught them to stick up for each other." He leans back, quiet for a moment. Then he says, "That's the main reason I feel bad about my bisexuality. Enid stands by me, but she only tolerates that. I guess it would be better if it weren't there—but it is!"

"It's not worth giving up?"

He shakes his head. "I don't think I could live without a man any more than I could live without a woman—I should say without my wife, because there is no other woman. Maybe it's just that with her I feel a real man."

"How do you define a real man?"

He considers that for a moment. "A man who doesn't let himself get pushed around."

"But you think homosexual activities aren't masculine?"

He shrugs. "I don't really consider myself a homosexual. I'm not one of those fags you see on TV or marching with gay groups."

"Then how do you feel when you're with another man?"

He moves back in his chair and looks uncomfortable. I pursue the question. "How do you feel?"

"Sex with another man is different. I get something completely different out of it. How can I explain it? Look, two years ago my father died and it shook me up, even though I hadn't seen much of him in the past few years, maybe because of that. He lived in California. But for a week after he died, after I came back from the funeral, I felt an over-whelming need for another man's body. It wasn't even on a sexual level. I just wanted to hold someone in my arms, to feel male skin against me." He is silent for a long moment.

"Your father's death really shook you up?"

He spreads his hands. "It sure did. We were always close. I remember as a kid I used to go to the hardware store and play with all the saws and hammers. He was pretty tolerant about that. I don't ever remember his getting mad or blow-ing up at me. He used to take me to baseball games, too. He was exactly what you'd expect a regular father to be."

He looks past me, momentarily lost in his memories. "He always came home on time and mother'd have the dinner table set. My older brother and I would be there, and there was the usual bickering—but he was around when I needed him."

"He sounds like he was a really nice guy."

"He was easygoing and quiet. He was older than my friends' fathers, a calm, even-tempered, old-fashioned family man."

"Were you able to talk to him?"

"We didn't have much time for that. He wasn't much of a talker, but I never missed it."

"Was he affectionate?"

"I guess so." He hesitates. "When I was a little kid he never liked me to crawl up on his lap."

"You said that when your father died you felt the need for a man."

"Christ, yes! I wanted a man. I wanted the feel of a man. It was so bad that I invented a business trip and went to a nearby city where there's a club baths."

"What's that?"

"Well—" he gestures vaguely. " 'Club' is kind of a euphe-mism for a homosexual bath. Almost every big city has one, at least one. You know what the baths are?"

"Yes."

"Well, I spent two days there. They have food machines in the lounge, and I ate my meals there, too, mostly Hostess Twinkies and coffee. I didn't even go back to my hotel room. It was like I couldn't get enough, no matter how much I had."

"Enough sex?"

Frowning, he shakes his head. "Not sex, really. I don't know if I came three times in those two days. It was just the need to hold another body in my arms, to make love to another man."

"What did you get out of it?"

He shakes his head. "I don't really know why, but the feel of a man's body next to mine is very comforting. I guess it makes me feel secure."

"Do you mean you want to hold someone, or be held?"

There's a long pause while he shifts uncomfortably. "To be perfectly honest, I like to be held."

"When you talk about the need to make love to another man, I get the feeling that you're using the word 'love' in a different way."

"I don't love the men I have sex with. I may like them and have affection for them, but I really wouldn't use the word 'love.' " He pauses for a moment. "To me, the word 'love' has to have time with it. You don't meet someone and fall in love. That's infatuation. Love is loyalty. That's what I get from my wife."

"And when you say you make love to a man?"

He smiles. "I'm using the word only in its sexual sense."

"Did holding a man in your arms, making love to him in the baths, help?"

He nods. "Yes. It was better afterward. I went home and things were very loving with my wife." He looks around the coffee shop and signals the waitress. "You want something else?"

"No, I'm fine."

While the waitress gets our check, I ask, "In what way was it better afterward? When you went home to your wife?"

"I guess somehow I felt more at ease with myself. My father's death didn't hurt so much. I don't think it was just because I was satisfied sexually—or maybe it was. I don't know."

"Does this happen often, that you feel better coming home after a sexual encounter?"

"Sometimes." He purses his lips. "It makes things smoother between me and my wife. I guess it's because I go out of my way to please her more."

"Do you feel guilty about your encounters away from home?"

He looks at me sharply. "I should, I guess. The point is, I get different things out of sex with a man and sex with a woman, and I need them both."

The check comes and I reach for it, but he waves me aside. "This is on me. I'm on an expense account." Outside it's a cool night, and we walk toward Third Avenue, then uptown.

We have here a man surrounding himself with a complete set of rationalizations for his behavior. He is basically a man torn by conflict who does not realize he is being torn. In order to hide this confusion from himself, he has erected a façade of being a happy family man who would do anything to keep his family together.

If we define bisexuality as the action of having sexual relations with both sexes at the same time, this man would fit the definition. On the other hand, it isn't that simple. It is possible for a person to have sex with both male and female partners and yet be basically homosexual. When this is the case, one side of his sexual life is being used for a cover-up. Many people who are gay claim that the bisexual is basically homosexual, but merely covering up his homosexuality by saying he is interested in members of the opposite sex and even going so far as having sex with them. They claim that when the person can admit and face his basic homosexual orientation, he will give up his bisexuality and "come out" into the homosexual world. When this is true, it is often very difficult for the basically homosexual person to "face it" because he has erected a superstructure to cover up his homosexuality, and the abandoning of this superstructure brings about a short-circuiting of his entire life.

I believe this to be true of Clark. He gives lip service to being interested in women, but claims he can't go to bed with them because it would be a betrayal of his wife and he wouldn't want to upset her. When asked what he would do if he had to give up men for some reason or another, he is very hesitant about his ability to do this. Further, he constantly stresses that he is a "family man" with all the obligations that implies, yet he spends every minute he can looking for men. It is difficult to conceive of Clark as having a basic drive toward being a family man except in name only. It would appear he grew up in a family where the wife and children were of paramount importance. He is attempting to fit into this image, but in so doing, he is being torn apart.

During the interview he constantly strives to paint a solid family portrait, and yet this is not what comes across. Before his marriage he tried to be honest with his fiancée and confessed his desire for men. It is almost as if once he had made this confession, it relieved him of all the responsibility of any real sexual dedication to his wife. When he speaks of his sexual life, his drive is certainly for men, and his sexual drive toward his wife appears to be minimal. One gets the feeling he is going through the motions with her and yet telling himself that he has a great life with her sexually. In this case it seems quite contradictory.

His wife is quite unhappy about his sexual activities with men, and it comes out in many ways. She keeps after him about his weight and tells him she doesn't understand how the other men can make love to a fat man. She nags him about working about the house, which is usually a sign that things are not going too well at home. It is true she stood by him during the two episodes in which he was publically confronted with bisexual complications. He takes this as a sign that his wife loves him, but it can also have an entirely different meaning. Perhaps his wife stood by him because her commitment to the marriage as a marriage was strong enough to allow her to support her husband in a time of stress. It is also possible she can't get out of the marriage for financial reasons.

Clark says it is much better to have homosexual relations than to commit adultery. This is an interesting definition of adultery! He goes further in his rationalization process and says it is a good way to keep the family together. In other words, he attempts to turn it into a positive value for the marriage. In this case it is clearly untrue, since his wife does not like his activities and takes her dislike out on him in many ways. In other cases we have examined, this was not the case. Some couples describe their bisexual activities as a means by which they became much more honest with each other, therefore bringing them closer together in all aspects of their lives. This is certainly not true with Clark and his wife. He says he would like to be honest, but he doesn't discuss his homosexual activities with his wife. Also, when he got seriously involved with one man, it played havoc with his home life. He described it as a regular *Back Street* where they had to sneak around and hide all their activities. Every reader who has had an extramarital relationship will recognize this type of feeling and activity. Clark is kidding himself if he thinks that bisexuality keeps his marriage together or contributes to it in any way.

Clark says he can't get enough sex, that he could have it every hour on the hour if he could find enough men or enough time. Some men make statements like this because they have very little sex and are indulging in a sort of fantasy, but in Clark's case, he is quite serious. In effect, he is not really describing a sexual drive even if he thinks he is. There is some other underlying need that he is attempting to satisfy through an exploitation of sex. His actions are like those of a person who feels unloved and constantly eats in order to satisfy his desire to be loved. We do not have a great deal of evidence about what underlying need Clark has that leads him on his never-ending sexual quests, but we do have some clues.

He said that when his father died he had an overpowering need to be held by a man and threw himself into a frenzy of homosexual activity. It is not so much his desire to hold another man but the need to be held himself that is important. He never mentions this in regard to his wife or any other woman, but this need runs through almost all his descriptions of men. When he gets this love he is satisfied, but only for a short time, and then he must seek it again. It is as if he needs to be constantly held by a man.

Clark describes his father as a family man dedicated to his children. He says his father was there when he was needed. Many hours were spent in talking with his father and sharing his hardware store with him. As good as this was, something appeared to be lacking, and lacking so strongly that it affected Clark's sexual patterns. He got little if any physical attention from his father—the kind of attention most fathers give to their children, letting them climb up on their laps, playing horsy with them, and the like. In many cases this would not cause any serious damage, but I believe in Clark's case it played a primary part in determining his need to be held by a man. This need continues to this day. No matter how much he is held by men, it is not enough, and it is not enough because it does not supply the physical fatherly love that Clark needs.

Clark will never find this love because as he states, he doesn't love the men he sleeps with. If he is seeking love through physical contact, but keeps himself from falling in love with the men, it is clear he will never satisfy his need for love. It is a vicious circle: the more he is held by men, the more his need is activated, and without the love he is seeking, the more frustrated that need becomes.

People often re-create their early childhood families in their own marriages, and this seems, in part at least, to be true of Clark. It appears his wife and his mother were a great deal alike. He said his mother always had the food on the table and was really a devoted family person. This is the same impression we have of Clark's wife. One gets the feeling that the children were extremely important to Clark's mother and father, and certainly this is true with his wife. In fact, it is so important to Clark's wife that she has not forced him to come to grips with his sexual confusion.

Basically, Clark has a very low image of himself. He says he adopts any role that is necessary in his sexual activities because it is all a game. This may sound logical, but it also implies he doesn't feel there is enough inside himself to take a position and let others relate to that position. One gets the distinct impression that he is playing a series of roles. One is the conservative family man with the nice little house in the suburbs. Another is the devoted husband who never cheats on his wife. Another is the devoted father. At the same time, he plays the role of the active "lover about town." Where is there room for Clark himself? There isn't—he is lost.

Unfortunately, this man appears to be basically homosexual without being able to face it, and to be using a series of rationalizations to hide this fact from himself. In the course of his life there will most likely be some external event that will bring his "bisexual" life out into the open, thus destroying the façade he has so carefully erected.

4
Angela

Angela lives on the second floor of a walkup on Chicago's North Side. There is a careless, disarranged look to the apartment, but it's comfortable and lived-in. It's the sort of place where you sit down and automatically put your feet up on the coffee table. There are stacks of books and magazines on the chairs, and no two pieces of furniture really match, yet they all look as if they belong together. There are mounted squares of fabric hung like pictures on the walls, and their bold, striking colors modify the room's drabness.

A wire-haired terrier greets me, frantically barking at first, then tearing from one end of the apartment to the other and back, yipping with delight. Apologetically, Angela says, "He loves company. He gets out so seldom."

I sit down, and the terrier, named Bias because "he walks on the bias," brings me a toy bone to play with. I tug at one end while he growls and hangs onto the other. "Is he a good watchdog?"

"He's fierce with other dogs, but a pussycat with people."
She puts her hand down, and he drops the bone and runs to
her to be petted. "Mainly he's company. I do most of my
work at home, and he's nice to have around. Very undemanding."

"As good as a man around the house?"

She smiles and nods at a chair. "Sit down. Better than a
man, or a woman. He doesn't demand anything."

I sit down in a worn but comfortable armchair, and Bias
comes trotting to me with another toy. "Is that so important,
not demanding?"

She sits down across from me and lights a cigarette.
"When you value your privacy the way I do, it is important.
I don't think I could ever live with anyone again."

I watch her draw in a deep breath of smoke and exhale it
slowly. She's well into her forties, a good-looking woman
with dark, fluid eyes and heavy unplucked brows. She has
high cheekbones and jet-black hair pulled back into a low
bun. She's wearing a brightly colored caftan, and she tucks
her bare feet under her in the chair. She's tall and solidly
built without being too heavy, and she moves with an easy
grace. "You've been married?" I ask.

"Twice. I was married at seventeen, before I knew which
side was up."

"Did your parents oppose it?"

"No. My father was pleased about it, even though I was
still a kid."

"Why was he pleased?"

She shrugs. "My father liked Bob. He was a real all-
American stereotype. We were an Italian family trying to
fit in. We lived in the suburbs because that was supposed to
be a good place to raise kids—and I guess it was, if you
wanted a certain type of kid."

"What type was that?"

"You know." She gestures vaguely. "A good, clean, acceptable type. All I ever wanted was to fit in with the rest. There weren't any Italian kids in our class, so I hung out with the Wasps. I did the whole cardigan, skirt, and string of pearls bit, and I hated myself because I had this Italian face."

"And your parents?"

She smooths out her caftan, staring at the design. Her voice is bitter. "All they wanted was to escape their own background. I remember once I got into a fight with a teacher and I had to stay after school. I felt the teacher was wrong, but when I told my mother, she bawled me out and said I was acting too 'Italian' by talking back. It's a funny thing. I guess ethnic groups either love their own kind and make little enclaves, or they move away and try desperately to integrate. My parents knocked themselves out. They even avoided Italian food." She stands up abruptly and crumples the empty cigarette pack. "Where the hell did I put that damned carton?" She hesitates. "They would bawl me out for using my hands when I talked."

She finds the cigarettes and sits down, lighting one. "I wasn't kidding anyone. The kids all knew what I was. Once, in an argument, one of them called me a wop. I came home crying, and typically, my mother's answer was to tell me I I had been too emotional. Translation, too foreign. A wop! My God, I'm past forty, but I still get upset if I use my hands during an argument."

She sits down and draws in a deep breath of smoke, letting it out slowly. "I felt out of it. I knew what I was, but they made me so ashamed."

"Who?"

"My mother, my father." She shakes her head. After a moment, she says very softly, "My father was a very handsome man, big and blond. He was from the north of Italy. They're like that up there."

"And your mother?"

"Her family came from the south." She pushes her hair

back. "I have her coloring. As a kid I would have given anything to look like him. And that's funny, because when I
go back to Italy, I'm going to Naples. I'm happier there, in
the south."

"Are you going to live in Italy?"

She laughs. "I hope so. I've been there three times, and
I'm trying to scrape up the money for another trip. I'm really
into the whole Italian bit now. I guess it's a reaction."

"What did your father do for a living?"

"He inherited Mom's family business, a contracting firm,
and he ran it well. My brother runs it now, but Dad was
always a little ashamed of it, and he was disappointed when
my brother went right into the business from high school.
You see, Dad came over when he was just a kid. He never
went to college, but he was big on education and read a
tremendous amount. He had one room—his study, he called
it—and he used to spend every evening in it reading."

"Did he stress education?"

"Not for me. But he did for my brother. Not that he ever
said anything about my going to school. I could tell he
thought it was a waste."

"And your mother?"

"She was into housecleaning. She did everything for my
father and brother. Before they had a shirt off, she had it
into the washing machine and ironed and back in the closet.
With me, she was always after me to pick up, be neat, act
like a lady. She made me shave my legs before I had any
hair on them! And the house. She had slipcovers on the slipcovers. The living room was like foreign territory. We
weren't allowed in except on special occasions."

She looks around the apartment and laughs ruefully. "I
guess you could make a good case for this place being such
a mess. Maybe I'm still fighting her."

I let her mull that over for a while, then I ask, "And how
did they get along, your parents?"

"Well, on the outside it was all smooth, but they never seemed to have much to say. Mostly my mother was involved with the house, and Dad with the business, or he was in his study reading. I never realized that things weren't so great until after we got the TV. Then it became pretty obvious."

"What do you mean?"

"Well, they didn't really like spending any time together. When they had to be with each other, they communicated with a kind of shorthand—I mean, on the surface what they said was fine, but underneath there was all this tension."

"What kind of tension?"

She turns in her chair uneasily. "Well, how can I explain? It was like they talked when the kids were around because they had to. They were just as happy not to talk, and when we got the TV, the family sort of split up. I mean, here was my mother and brother glued every night to the TV, and Daddy and I were in his study. I'd be doing my homework and he'd be reading. Lots of times we'd just talk. We had some wonderful evenings together."

"And you were married at seventeen?"

She sighs, as if reluctant to put aside the memory of her father. "Yes. I was a cheerleader—that's integrating! And Bob was a football star. Oh, hell, not a star really. He wasn't all that good, but he was tall and blond. Neither of us knew what we were doing, and we were both virgins." She shakes her head. "Don't ask me how, but the marriage lasted for seven years. Maybe it was because we were both too dumb to split up."

"Was it bad?"

"Not bad, just dull and absolutely meaningless." Bias jumps up in her lap, and she scratches him behind the ears absently. "Don't get me wrong. Bob was a very considerate person, in all ways—sexually, too. I was a housewife, because in my experience that was all women were. I kept a nice house and cleaned and cooked and tried to live up to every-one's expectations."

"What about your own expectations?"

"I didn't really have any. I knew something was wrong, but I didn't know what. On the surface, everything seemed fine. Bob was a commercial artist and had a good job for a few years. It's funny. I had always fooled around with art, but I never touched it while Bob was working." She gestures at the framed fabric on the walls. "Those are my designs."

I admire them. They're bright and bold and the colors are all in startling combinations. I realize that she must have also designed the fabric of her caftan.

"What made you give it up?"

She shrugs. "I suppose I didn't want to compete with him. Not that it mattered. He lost his job and things got very tight financially, and I began working as a waitress now and then, especially when the bills piled up. It's funny. Things seemed better when I was working, at least to me."

"And Bob?"

She shakes her head. "I guess somehow I must have failed him. Looking back now, it's not too hard to understand. I never finished high school and I was a kid, in every way. I was a kid playing at being a woman, and I guess he wanted a real wife, whatever that is."

"What did you want?"

"I don't know." She grinds out her newly lit cigarette and lights another. "I just knew I didn't want what I had. When Bob told me he wanted a divorce, I went through the mo-tions of being heartbroken, but I was honestly relieved. I felt as if I were being given a second chance, being let out of prison."

"What did you do?"

Disgustedly, she says, "I blew the whole thing. Oh, for a few months it was fine. I didn't go home, thank heavens. I got a full-time job as a waitress—it was all I knew how to do—but I started school again. I really didn't regret the marriage breaking up, but then, within six months I was married again. Don't ask me why. I suppose marriage was the only thing I knew. You know, I can't even remember what he looked like, Ralph—at least I remember his name!"

"How long did it last?"

"A year. It was a total disaster. I don't even like to talk about it." She pushes the dog off her lap. "I decided that that was the end of marriage as far as I was concerned." She laughs. "I've come close a few times, but I always escaped at the last minute."

"What did you do after that?"

"I finished high school, for one thing, and I began to go to college at night. I worked days. It was tough, but I enjoyed it. I went through a few waitress jobs, then landed a cushy spot as hostess in a fancy nightclub. The pay was good, but more important, I felt alive."

"What about your sex life?"

She laughs. "In a job like that, there were always men. I've never had trouble with sex. I enjoy it, and always did. In fact, the only good thing about both my marriages was the sex." She's thoughtful for a moment. "I think my bisexuality just evolved out of my sexuality."

Puzzled, I ask, "What do you mean?"

"It's just that I was attracted to women and women were attracted to me." She hesitates. "Actually, the first bisexual experience I had was with a man and a woman."

"How did that happen?"

"Let's see. I was working at the club, and when my shift was over, one of the girls who worked there came in with her boy friend and we all went to a nearby bar. They were sitting on either side of me, and I realized that they were both coming on. It was a strange feeling, but I enjoyed it.

Then they insisted that I come see their new apartment. I knew what was happening, but I thought, 'Wow! Let's see what it's all about.' So I went along."

She smiles reminiscently. "It was good. Sexually, sure, but more than sexually."

"How do you mean, more?"

"Well, the three of us shared something. I don't know how to explain it, but maybe it's that sharing that was so great. Sure, we'd had something to drink, but not enough to account for what we felt."

"What did you feel?"

"There's a tenderness to sex with a woman that you don't find with a man, and there's a quality in a man's lovemaking that you don't find with a woman." She laughs. "Having both together just blew my mind."

"Did you see them again?"

She shakes her head. "I didn't want to. Maybe it was too good. I don't know, but I went back to men after that, for a few months at least. Then for a while things were very bad."

"What happened?"

A surprising sadness suddenly comes into her voice and her eyes seem full. "My father died. I was home on a visit— he had been very sick—and I walked into his room one morning and found him dead." She bites her lips. "My mother had gotten up and dressed, and was making breakfast. She never knew."

"You didn't stay at home?"

"Christ, no. I never considered it. Anyhow, it was after that that I had my first long affair with a woman." She looks around the apartment. "I'm seeing a woman now, more or less exclusively. It's a very nice relationship. One of the most honest I've had."

"Are you monogamous in sexual relationships?"

She shrugs. "No. Only in my marriages. Maybe that was

one of the things wrong with them, seeing one person exclusively. Now Stella and I have a relationship, but I still do have affairs—or I'd call them encounters."

"And other women?"

"No. Neither of us sees other women, probably because we satisfy each other completely in that direction. We're both very happy. Stella has the keys to this apartment, and she comes and goes as she pleases. She knows that she might come in and find a guy here, but that doesn't bother her, and it doesn't bother me."

"Do you find you respond more physically to a man than to a woman?"

"I don't think it's the man or woman as much as the person. I think both the male and the female body can be beautiful, and in all honesty, one doesn't turn me on any more than the other."

She stands up and stretches, and I become aware of her body under the caftan, tall and big, but graceful and well-proportioned. "Can I make you some coffee?"

"Thanks." I follow her into the kitchen, a pleasant, open room in a state of great disorder. She measures out some coffee beans and grinds them in a mill attached to the wall, adding a stick of cinnamon. The coffee, once it is brewed, is rich and pungent.

"I think, since the women's movement, women have become friends. They've learned how. They didn't know how twenty years ago. They were catty to each other, in competition for husbands really. Now you can be friends with another woman without using her. We all tended to use each other."

We sit down with our coffee at a round oak table, and she brushes a pile of knitting off onto a chair. "It was always pretty girl and ugly girl. The pretty girl got the men, and the ugly girl had to fall back on a brain or a job. The women's movement has taught us that getting the man isn't the be-all and end-all of life. I'm pretty happy without a man, and so are a lot of my friends."

She breaks off suddenly and smiles, and I realize that in some ways her face is quite beautiful. "Am I lecturing?"

Smiling, I say, "I'm used to that. My wife has trained me."

She laughs, and I ask curiously, "Don't you feel that you sometimes want a man around?"

"Want?" She frowns. "Not in the sense of possession. If I need a man, one is always easy to find. If I want to live with one, that's easy, too. But the point is, I can also live with a woman, or alone, and still think I'm worth something."

"You're very pro women's movement."

"Oh, there are things about it that I don't like. Women made a great mistake in imitating the oppressor, men. I don't want to be like a man. I wouldn't know how to be like a man. I think that's impossible." She reaches back to tuck in a strand of hair, and the gesture is completely feminine. "We should try to develop our own skills, whatever they are, and conquer our own fields, whatever they are."

She pauses. "You know, there's a difference to all sex. Some men are aggressive and others are gentle, and some women are gentle and some aggressive. Sometimes I'm aggressive with a woman, and sometimes I'm aggressive with a man. Maybe it's the kind of sex that's different." She considers a moment. "Or the frequency. With a man, there's more sex than with a woman. A man is more easily aroused, and sex comes easier—but the intensity, the fantasy, the orgasm are all the same."

"What fantasies do you have with a man?"

She smiles, a very introspective smile. There is a touch of Mona Lisa in it. "I think of other men, almost always. And sometimes I think of them both together with me. It's funny." She cradles her coffee cup in her hands. "I fantasize very dominant men, very aggressive men."

"And with women?"

Again the smile. "I guess the fantasies are different. I think of the women as softer and yielding. I always fantasize myself as the aggressor. With a man, I like to think of myself as powerless, unable to resist."

"But you find the orgasm the same?"

She shrugs. "Women have to work at their orgasm, no matter who they're screwing." She shakes her head. "Men are usually concerned with their erection and their performance, but then, I've had some men lovers who were very considerate."

"And bisexual men?"

"I've only had affairs with one or two bisexual men. I prefer completely heterosexual men, and heterosexual women. I've never had an affair with a bull dike, because they fight with me."

"But if you had an affair with a woman, wouldn't she be bisexual, not heterosexual?"

"Yes . . . " She sips her coffee thoughtfully. "But basically I think the women I like call themselves heterosexual."

"Do you see yourself as heterosexual?"

"No. I consider myself bisexual."

"But how would you have an affair with a heterosexual woman, short of seducing her, unless she was also bisexual?"

She considers. "Well, take the situation now. Stella had never had an affair with a woman, and yet she seduced me. I was very surprised because she's much younger than I am. She lived a heterosexual life, but she thought of herself as a lesbian because her fantasies were all about women. She was a heterosexual who's now bisexual. A lot of women who've started to experiment with bisexuality were heterosexual before. I've been experimenting, too. Up until about five years ago most of my bisexual experiences were with couples, men and women."

"There were other experiences after that first one?"

"Oh, yes." Dryly, she says, "Since it didn't drive me home to slice my wrists or douche with Lysol."

"Did it upset you in any way?"

"I giggled a lot. No, it didn't upset me. In fact, I felt rather good about it. It was an exciting experience, and eye-opening." She stirs her coffee thoughtfully. "There have been periods when I was actually asexual."

"What do you mean?"

"I gave it up altogether for a while."

"Why?"

She looks up at me, her dark eyes very liquid. "Everything about it, about sex, had gotten so free and meaningless—that was about six or seven years ago. It got to the point where I was just screwing anybody. You'd meet somebody on the street or at a party and think, 'He looks familiar,' and then realize that you had tumbled into bed with him after some party. It got to be sick, too much. I guess I overreacted. I became a recluse for about nine months. I stopped going out and I just stayed home."

"What were you doing then?"

"I had finished college and I was studying fabric design. I guess I always had some talent, but when my first husband was trying so hard to make a go of art, I just buried whatever talent I had. Later, I began to do sketches for friends, and then I met a guy in the fabric business who told me I had a real flair and suggested I do some designs for him. I ended up designing fabrics. That's why I first went to Italy, to Forence, for ideas. I was working for a Finnish designer when I gave up sex."

"Gave up sex?"

"Completely, and I wasn't the only one. Most of my friends were fed up."

"Why?"

She hesitates, then blurts out, "It was lie, all the freedom."

"Sexual freedom?"

"Yes. The promiscuity was ridiculous. I began to understand it was much better when people got to know each other. We were like faceless people going through our lonely lives. When I realized that, it was a big turning point for me."

"What happened then?"

"I came back to having sex with people I really liked, regardless of what their sex was, and I think I've been there ever since." She looks at me earnestly. "Don't get me wrong. I feel this is right for me, but I realize other people have other needs. My feeling is that everyone must manage his own sexuality. You have to get straight what's good for you. I wouldn't try to convert anyone to bisexuality, but I think that homosexual men miss a lot by confining their sex to men, and the same for homosexual women."

"I'm not sure I understand that."

She leans forward across the table. "Well, look. When I meet a gay man who's never slept with a woman, I think, how do you know you don't like it if you don't try it—and women who are exclusively homosexual should try the experience of sharing the warmth and love of a man. It's a beautiful experience with either sex. I know."

Her face seems very soft, very maternal, as she talks, and I ask, "Have you ever thought in terms of another marriage, of children?"

Without hesitating, she says, "No. Honestly, no. What I want to do with my life now is to travel, to see more of the world. I like to travel. I like to live in other countries. The customs, the language—they're all exciting to me. I spent ten months in Italy last year, in Naples. I felt as if I had finally come home. I gave English lessons and worked in a poster shop and art gallery down by the port. I made enough money to live on—just. You can live very cheaply if you're a vegetarian."

"Are you?"

"More or less. I ate once a day, one meal, and I walked a lot and saw so much. I loved it." She leans back and spreads her arms out. "I could get along. I didn't need a steady job if I was willing to settle for a little less. Now, when I need money, I sell some designs to my friend, the guy in fabrics." She gestures around the apartment. "This is fine for me. I don't need much, and I have no great attachments. It's easy to take off for Europe. The only trouble is Bias."

The dog lifts his head at his name and cocks it to one side. "I didn't take him with me last time."

"What did you do?"

"I have a friend I left him with. He's gay and makes no demands, and he loves the dog. He and Bias got on perfectly while I was gone, but next time I'm taking Bias along."

"Why did you leave Italy?"

"I had to renew my visa. They get a little nervous when you have a job or work permit or apply for residency."

"And you couldn't see doing all this with a partner, a husband or a family?"

She laughs and gets up to pour herself another cup of coffee. "I don't think I'm that interested in building a life with someone else, no matter what sex. That's a girlish, romantic concept. I was married twice, without much joy, just all the trouble and dullness. I've had it, and I don't want it again. I don't want to roll over every morning and see the same person."

She sits down and stirs her coffee. "For me the ideal thing would be a friend who has his or her place and his or her life—and would let me have mine." She sips a bit of coffee and frowns, her brows a heavy bar across her dark eyes. "I think the most terrible thing about my parents' marriage was that they felt they had to stay together. I think my father lived in a trap."

"Would you have to be caught in the same trap?"

"I won't find out. When I first started this affair with Stella, I looked on it as an interim thing. I was waiting until I would have a real affair with a man. That, to me, seemed the proper way of things. Then I thought, that's crazy. What difference does it make if my relationship is with a woman instead of a man? Now I realize my relationship must be with a person, man or woman, and Stella is that person." She falls silent for a moment, then looks up at me. "Or I can make it alone. Each man is an island."

"Do you really believe that?"

"I think so." Her face is thoughtful for a moment. "I really think a person should be self-contained." She smiles suddenly. "But I might build a bridge to another island— or take a boat. The point is, I'm me, and I'm going to be me and do what I want, and what I want is complete freedom in any relationship. That's where it's all at. If you really love someone, you leave him his freedom. That's the most precious thing you can give. If you try to entangle someone in your life, you're just trapping him."

"And you feel that's what happened to you?"

"Oh, it did. I didn't learn, even after two marriages. I went into a relationship with a guy for three years, and it was a complete trap under the name of love." Bitterly, she says, "That's where I learned about woman's work and man's work. I did the shit work, and he went out to see if there were any Indians on the horizon. We never found any in Chicago, but if we had, he would have been ready." She shakes her head. "I never got into that bind again, and I never want to."

"Do you think it always has to be that way?"

"Sure. Most people want to live together when they find each other, and once they're together they want to change their partner. I find that men are always trying to change me. They think of me as some kind of wild animal they have

to tame, and I don't think I'm wild at all. I consider myself
a very sedate person. They're attracted to the fact that I'm
gregarious, but they want me gregarious only with them, if
that's possible."

"Don't women have the same desire to possess and
change?"

"I don't find that Stella has it, but I've had relationships
with women where they've played bitches, played the tricks
on me they were supposed to play on men, the tricks they
learned at mama's knee." Her voice is heavy with contempt.
"When men say they can't understand women, they mean
women like that, and I agree. I can't understand them
either."

She stands up abruptly and clears the table, clattering the
dishes into the sink. "Come on inside. I'll clean up later."
Bias jumps up eagerly and follows us into the living room,
ready for a new game. In her chair, Angela says, "I think
that women have had a rough deal. They're told they only
get their identity when they capture some poor slob in
marriage. If a woman is a doctor, it isn't enough. Hell,
one of the best friends my parents had was a woman doctor.
She was incredible. She had a car, a summer house, an important practice and hospital appointment, but my mother
pitied her. Why? My mother would say, 'She's ugly, poor
thing.' My mother was a very attractive woman. She had
my coloring, even my nose, but she was beautiful, and she
never did anything except take care of her house and wait
on my father and brother. It made me think and it opened
my eyes. I'm smart, and I'm not ugly, so the two don't have
to go together, and if they do, which is more important? I'd
rather be that doctor than my mother if I had a choice.
Any day."

"What does your mother think of the life you lead?"

"She doesn't know too much about it. I've thrown a lot
of hints at her about my bisexuality, but she doesn't pick

anything up. Still, she has been understanding, more so since my father died. I think she's grown up a lot. It's funny, a few years ago I got careless and found I was pregnant. For a while I thought I'd have the baby, and she was very supportive. Very. She never once preached or scolded, but she rarely came around."

"You were alone then?"

"Yes. By choice. I wanted the baby to be entirely mine. It's strange. I never believed in the complete change women go through in pregnancy, but I would burst into tears when I'd see a leaf fall down, things like that."

"Did you have the baby?"

No. I was pregnant four and a half months, then I had a late abortion. But I enjoyed the part of the pregnancy I experienced."

"What changed your mind?"

She shrugs. "I thought it would be better for everybody at that point. It wasn't a very rational decision to have it. I was going to leave the city and not tell anyone the baby was illegitimate, but now I wouldn't do that." Her voice became challenging. "If I had a child, I'd have it where I lived and everyone could accept it or not. But I couldn't think that way then. I was so vulnerable. I couldn't make an intelligent decision, and the baby was an accident. I really wasn't prepared to have it. Now things are different. Now I think I'd have the baby and enjoy it."

"Wouldn't it cut your freedom down?"

Quickly, she says, "A child doesn't possess you. I don't think it would have hindered my life. It might mean I'd stay home more, work more at free-lance designing. I certainly wouldn't have ended up with a baby on welfare. I'm a survivalist. I'm always going to make it—it would just have meant a different way of making it." Thoughtfully, she adds, "A child's not a burden forever. They grow up. They do things. They go to school." She hesitates, and her

voice becomes tight. "At the time I couldn't do it. I wasn't
strong enough. Some women have done it, and in a few
years more women will. A lot of women don't want husbands, and a lot of men don't want babies."

The subject bothers her, and I try to change it. "Are you
involved in any of the gay movements?"

She shakes her head. "I'm very suspicious of movements.
I've seen so many of them get screwed up or bogged down,
and I don't see why the whole gay movement is any different."

"Are you a political person?"

She pats the back of her hair and says, "I'm a very political
person, in spite of my suspicion of movements."

"Are you left, right, or center?"

She laughs. "I'm an anarchist. I believe in the least
amount of government possible."

"Don't you believe in laws?"

"There doesn't have to be a law that says that murder is
bad. Murder is a crime of passion, and you can't make laws
against crimes of passion. You shouldn't steal. Fine. I believe
in that. But if people steal in spite of the law, what good is
it? Even speeding on the highway. People speed whether
or not there's a law."

She reaches for her cigarettes and tries to light one, making two or three futile attempts with the match. "Damn!"
She takes her cigarette to the kitchen and lights it from
the gas, then stands in front of me. "The work force in this
country has people pushing things from the in box to the
out box, and I don't think it's necessary. Everybody could
do all the office work needed in a four-hour day. Maybe it's
different with real workers, fruit pickers and laborers, but
then the pay should be adjusted." She sits down abruptly.
"I think capitalism is the worst society you can live under
if you're not a capitalist." She takes a deep drag on the
cigarette and stubs it out, then looks at it ruefully. "I waste

more than I smoke, but I guess that's healthy. I think the biggest problem in this country is apathy. There's so much selfishness in the way people conduct their lives, and I hate it."

She reaches for another cigarette, then looks at the pack and resolutely puts it aside. "I like Italy. Everyone was involved. They have incredible demonstrations, and you feel so nationalistic after one of them. A couple of bombs go off, and there are fights between the Fascists and the Communists—it's all like theater."

"Do you read much?"

She reaches out to touch a pile of books on one of the chairs. "I spend most of my time reading. Right now it's Huxley and Orwell. They had so much foresight. It's amazing how pertinent they are, more now than when they were written. I don't read much fiction, but I like history." She smiles, remembering. "I guess I inherited that from my father. He used to read every night—American history. He had a fine mind." She nods at a shelf behind me, and I turn to find it piled with new books, most of them in Italian. "My friends in Italy keep sending me books on ancient Rome. Someday I'll read them all—there are so many things I want to do." She points to some of the framed fabrics on the walls. "I want to get into natural dyes in my prints. It's amazing how soft and subtle natural dyes can be."

"What are your friends like?"

"I haven't many friends, but the few I have are good ones, and they think the way I do. Most of them are artists of one kind or another. Stella is a weaver, and my closest male friend is a sculptor. I used to be very social. There was always some kind of party going on, here or at a friend's. And I've been involved with consciousness-raising groups."

"What do you want out of life now?"

"What do I want?" She looks startled, then she frowns and reaches again for her cigarettes, this time lighting one with no trouble. "I want happiness, if there is such a thing." She draws in a deep breath of smoke and lets it trickle out. "And peace, peace and quiet. Maybe that's what I found in Naples. I'm not sure. I have to go back and find out. The first half of my life has been so filled with hostility and trauma—I want the rest of it to be calm.

"I want to be involved with people, but in a good way." She considers. "If I stay here, I think I'll continue to be active in the women's movement. I think it's taught me to like people more." She looks up at me a bit challengingly. "I don't think the movement has forced women into bed with each other. Some people involved with it say, 'If you're truly liberated, you have to go to bed with another woman,' but I think that's ridiculous. I think you can know someone without going to bed with her. If that's the only way you can get to know someone, then you're crazy."

She's silent for a long moment, then she adds, "You learn a different side of a person if you sleep with her, but I can't believe that to truly know someone, man or woman, you must sleep with them. I don't think that's true at all."

"And bisexuality? Has that come from the women's movement?"

"Not in my case, and not in a lot of others. I think a lot of bisexuality has come out of the similarity between men and women, today's similarity—the clothes, the long hair." She leans forward seriously. "There's not that much difference between a young man's body with long hair and a young girl with long hair. They're both hairless and small-breasted. Women no longer have tiny waists and large hips." She looks up and catches me smiling, and after a moment she smiles, too. "That's the over-forty generation speaking. Of course there's a difference, and I like the difference."

Bias, who has been sleeping under the table, suddenly erupts into life, barking furiously as a stray dog wanders below the window. He leaps up on the window ledge excitedly and Angela pats him, then grabs him up. "With a fierce protector like this, who needs a man around—on a permanent basis?"

She goes to the door with me, still holding the dog, and my last glimpse of her is like something in a medieval Italian painting, a calm, handsome face, but with a promise of passion behind her eyes.

When a psychologist listens to a patient or a person he is trying to understand, he builds up a picture of him bit by bit as he talks. The psychologist is like a painter who puts colors on the canvas a little at a time until in the end he has a complete picture. The painter may start out in one direction and as his picture builds find himself going in an entirely different direction. Let us follow the same process with Angela as I try to come to an understanding of her.

There is an old saying that you can't divorce a person from his surroundings, that is, his house is a reflection of what is inside him. Often the very disturbed person will live in a house that looks as if it has been hit by a cyclone. Angela's house seems to hang together in a very casual manner. Her chairs don't match, and things are carelessly strewn about the apartment. There is no attempt to impress the visitor with either her prosperity or her poverty. The pictures on the walls are done in bold colors. These surroundings tell us that Angela is content to let us see her casual approach to life, but that this casualness has within it the potential of strong emotional feelings. I would expect her to be a person of conviction and feeling.

Her feeling toward her dog is not unlike that of many other people—"Mainly he's company." There is, however, another element in her feeling that he is very undemanding. I would expect her not to like demanding people as well, and this indeed turned out to be true.

Her statement, "When you value your privacy the way I

do," gives us another indication of what type of person Angela is. She does not like people to demand things of her, and she wishes to be left alone to live her own life. Her not wishing to live with either a man or woman again is a clear indication that this is true.

According to Angela, her family was ashamed of being Italian and made every attempt to have Angela hide this from her friends. Families from a distinct ethnic background often take this attitude in an attempt to fit into the milieu in which they find themselves. Angela picked this up, and felt the most important thing for her was to fit in with the rest of the kids. Yet because she was obviously Italian she felt she didn't belong. She still feels part of this childhood conflict even today, because when she uses her hands she feels upset. This certainly was the beginning, as far as we can see from her conversation, of her conflict between fitting in and wanting to be left alone. Often, if one wants desperately to fit in and can't for some reason, the alternative is to withdraw. Angela did not withdraw, but she began to develop feelings of needing her privacy.

Her description of her father as a handsome man, big and blond, and the words she uses in describing him would make us look for clues in connecting her feelings toward her father and her relationships with men. This is not to fall into the trap of saying that she was looking for a father substitute, but it is saying that all children use their parents as models for their own behavior. If the models are appropriate to reality and are good models, it seems to work out well for the children in later life; but if the models are bad ones, then trouble often follows.

Angela's father was a hard-working, family-oriented man who spent a lot of time talking with her. She could feel close to him and feel he was interested in her; thus, there was nothing in their relationship that would turn her against men.

On the other hand, what she saw in the relationship between her father and mother could very well have colored her attitudes toward family life. She realized that her parents had no real marriage in the sense of sharing ideas or joint activities. She saw the tension that existed beneath the outward marital calm.

Often, when parents say proudly that they never fight in front of the children, they forget that the children can pick up the under-the-surface tension. In this case, the marriage was certainly not a good model for Angela to copy.

We would have to suspect that Angela's marriage at the age of seventeen might well have been partly explained by her desire to get out of the house. This is not at all unusual for children. Of course, we cannot overlook the fact that she describes her first husband as "tall and blond," like her father.

She describes this first marriage as dull and meaningless, which is exactly what she saw in her parents' marriage. She also made every attempt to emulate the role of her mother in her first marriage. She was a good housewife and kept everything neat and nice and, in her words, "tried to live up to everyone's expectations." Certainly she saw no professional competition between her father and mother, and she attempted to follow that model in her marriage. Unfortunately, it didn't work because they needed the money and she got a job. She still feels she might have failed her husband by not being a "real wife."

When she got divorced she felt relief at being let out of the prison. But the drive to follow the marriage model was too strong, and she found herself married again shortly afterward. The pattern began to repeat itself.

Angela's perception was that sex was the only thing that really worked in either of her marriages. We have to at least entertain the idea that if something is pleasurable, one will try to repeat it. On the other hand, all the other aspects of marriage did not appeal to her. The logical solution for her, then, would be to have the sex without the marriage. Indeed, this was her solution.

Her bisexuality started with a threesome—a replay of a family situation where she could be accepted by both the man and the woman. She recognized that there was more than sex involved in this first bisexual experience. It was the sharing that was so important to her. Perhaps we might say it was the sharing without all the responsibilities of marriage. As we saw, she spent a lot of time in threesome relations, but this didn't last because it didn't satisfy some need in Angela for a deeper meaning to sexual encounters. She didn't want "encounters," she wanted an affair with meaning.

It was right after her father died that she began her first serious affair with a woman. This sequence of events cannot be ignored. The very least we can say is that the death of her father released her from some sort of allegiance to her father, which in turn allowed her to relate openly to a woman on a sexual basis.

She describes herself as not monogamous in her sexual relations, but on one level this is not quite true. I have seen this pattern in many bisexuals. They will remain completely faithful to the member of their sex while playing around with the other sex. They seem to feel that sleeping with another person of the same sex is a betrayal. This is really monogamy within a bisexual setting. Angela is committed to her girl friend on an emotional level and would not betray that by having sexual relations with another woman.

There seems little question that Angela is a true bisexual in that she experiences no difficulty in relating sexually to both sexes. Also, she displays no hostility toward either sex, which means there is no indication of a basic homosexuality. In discussing her sexual attractions, she says she feels equally attracted to both sexes, and everything she says seems to substantiate this. With many other people who claim to be living a bisexual life I have found a basic homosexual pattern betrayed by deep distrust of the opposite sex. The often deeply felt and expressed contempt of male homosexuals toward women is well known, and if I find this in a person claiming to be a bisexual, I soon discover that the purported "bisexual" life is a cover-up for a homosexual existence.

When I talk with homosexuals, both male and female, many will tell me that bisexuality is merely a bus stop on the way to become "gay." This is certainly true in some cases, but it is equally untrue in many other cases. When I see a member of one sex taking on the characteristics of the other sex, I usually suspect there is not bisexuality but homosexuality. In the case of Angela, there is none of this, and as a matter of fact, she prides herself on having many feminine traits—or those traits that we culturally ascribe to women.

In any pattern of human behavior that deviates from the statistical norm, one should ask if this deviant pattern is a true resolution or if it is merely some type of escape. In many of the bisexuals we have interviewed it has obviously been an escape or an experimentation that will come to an end when some set of circumstances change. In the case of Angela, I do not believe this to be the case. She went through the usual questioning periods—the usual promiscuity—the doubts, despairs, and withdrawals we associate with the attempts to come to grips with a problem. As she said, she screwed everything in sight for a while, then she completely withdrew from sex for another period in her search for personal solutions to her life situation. In the end she came up with, for her, a viable lifestyle that is bisexual.

Angela did not want to be caught in the family trap as she

saw her father was or as her mother was, so she constructed a life without a trap—without marriage. To many people marriage is not a trap, but to Angela it was. At the same time, she was well adjusted enough to realize she could not live without warmth and love, so she adopted bisexuality as a means of obtaining this without the trap.

5

David and Ellen

David and Ellen's apartment is the top floor of a wooden, three-story converted private house in Brooklyn. David has met me at the subway and walked me to the house, and I climb the dingy, narrow stairs through two depressing floors to enter an astonishing apartment. The decoration is Victorian, but authentic Victorian, full-blown and overdone as only the genuine Victorians could manage. The walls are papered and paneled and hung with hundred-year-old pictures and prints. The drapes are velvet, edged with lace, the room openings are hung with portières. There is an overwhelming abundance of dark reds, greens, and blues in velvet and satin. The apartment is lit with soft lamps, the shades ruffled and flounced. The floors are carpeted, and where the wood shows, it is painted and stenciled.

I am overwhelmed, and I let David show me each room proudly, including the nursery with its Kate Greenaway prints, its old-fashioned crib, and collection of turn-of-the-century children's books. In the nursery, a young bearded friend in his twenties turns helplessly from a naked, one-year-old girl bounding happily in the crib. "David! How the hell do you put on these Pampers?"

I'm introduced to Roger, who has come over to baby-sit while David and I talk. Sherry, the baby, holds out her arms and I take her up and cuddle her. Then she reaches for her father, and in his arms looks at me flirtatiously over one chubby shoulder. She has blonde hair and blue eyes and is the prototype of every beautiful bouncing American baby. We flirt for a while, and then David puts her back in the crib and tells Roger, "Leave her without a diaper for a while. She gets her bottle in a half hour, and then she takes a nap."

We go into the bedroom to talk and shut the door against Sherry's deserted wail. The bedroom, with its canopied bed, is filled with decorator knickknacks including a dressmaker's dummy with an elegant red-velvet Victorian ball gown. David nods at it. "I made that for Ellen."

The apartment is different from anything I had expected. David is thirty-two, about six feet tall, well built, with blond hair and blue eyes. His face could pass in a crowd without distinction. His features are soft, his hair short and wiry. I make some admiring remarks about the apartment, and he smiles. "I did the whole thing myself because we didn't have any money, but I don't think I'd be interested in doing this as a career."

He talks easily, his words flowing together, and he uses his hands and face expressively as he talks. There is a charming, ingratiating air about him, and I have no trouble in getting him to talk. Settling down in a comfortable chair near mine, he tells me that until he was twenty-five he was completely uninterested in sex and with either men or women. "I was popular in high school, but I was a loner. I was friendly with everyone, but I had no real friends."

David dropped out of college in his first year and tried art school, then left that to work in the same art studio as his father.

"How did that work out?" I ask.

"You mean working with my father?"

"Yes."

"Not too well. My father's a good artist, and I could have learned a lot from him, but—well, I just had to accept the fact that I'd never be anything more than a kid to him. He just couldn't see me as an adult."

"What was he like?"

David considers. "Physically, very big. He was tremendously overweight and tall." There's a touch of resentment in his voice. "He was something of a bully, not only with me but with the men at work. He loved to push people around. He had my mother completely cowed. It's funny. It was during the worst week of my job, when things got to the point with dad, with his constant picking on me, where I knew I had to quit, that I had my first sexual experience with a man."

I say, "Tell me about it."

"Well, there isn't much to tell. I was hitching home from work, and a very well-dressed older man picked me up in his car. He was very nice, very concerned with what I was doing, my job—oh, I don't know. He wanted to hear about all the things I wanted to talk about and never could. I went home with him and—" He shrugs. "It upset me afterward, but I knew what I was getting into."

"How did it upset you?"

"I just felt rotten, let down, and I kept thinking, hell, was it worth doing something immoral like that for just a few minutes of pleasure?"

"You considered it immoral?"

"Very much so. I knew it was wrong, and I was afraid of becoming homosexual. Terrified, really."

He laughs. "I hadn't had any sexual experience with a woman, but I got a friend to introduce me to a girl who had a reputation for sleeping around. I spent a whole week's salary on her, and I finally got to sleep with her."

"Was it good?"

"It was awful! We had sex, but when I left her house I was sick, physically sick and sure I had some terrible venereal disease. I sweated out a whole month before I was convinced I wasn't sick."

"When did you have sex again?"

"It wasn't until a year later. I went into therapy after I quit my job because I had a terrible identification problem with men."

"Identification problem?"

"That's what the therapist called it. I was just afraid of men. I wouldn't go into any place, a gas station or a barbershop, where I'd be alone with a group of men. After about a year of therapy, I began to have sex with women, oh, not much, but at least there were no more homosexual experiences. Then I enlisted in the Army."

"With your fear of men?"

"I had gotten over a lot of that, and I guess I wanted to prove myself. I think I found my own strength in the service. I was accepted. In fact, I made sergeant, and that gave me a lot of confidence in myself."

"How did you meet your wife?"

"We met while I was in the Army, in Europe. She was working for the government. It's funny, my sexuality really began to develop in the service. I had sex with a lot of women."

"Were you married overseas?"

"No. Ellen and I had this real torrid love affair for three

weeks. Sex was great between us, and so was everything else." He jumps up and brings me a color photograph in an ornate frame. "This is Ellen, dressed up."

I look at a very lovely, slim woman in her thirties dressed in the red velvet gown, her arms and shoulders bare and her hair up in an Edwardian swirl. "Ellen is a year older than I am," David explains.

"How old were you when you were married?"

"I was twenty-five. We didn't want to be married overseas. Ellen's parents live in Indiana, and mine in California. After my discharge we flew to New York, and we were married here, without my parents or hers."

"Why?"

He shakes his head. "I love my parents and I try to deal with them on a mature level, but they always put me in a child's role, especially my father. He just won't accept the fact that I'm an adult. My parents would have found a way to louse things up. My mother's always been possessive. I was her little darling, and nobody was ever good enough for me. As a kid she wouldn't let me play with the other kids because they weren't 'good enough.' In school none of the girls I dated were up to her standards, whatever the hell those standards were. I knew she would have found some way to screw up the marriage—and I didn't want that. We flew to California after the wedding, and as it was, Ellen and my mother got into a terrible argument about what I'd do with my life. Finally, we just picked up and came East. They didn't talk to us for years, but now we're on passable terms."

"How has the marriage worked out?"

"Well, that was in 1969, and for two years I was completely faithful to Ellen. We had a good marriage and a very active sex life, though I realize now it was kind of dull."

"How do you mean, dull?"

He shrugs. "I suppose what I mean is it didn't live up to my fantasy life. Anyway, after two years I got involved with a man again—in a homosexual situation."

"How did that happen?"

He thinks for a moment. "Ellen was working as an executive secretary. She's really good and never has any trouble getting a job." He sounds bitter now. "I'd get a job, usually a lousy one, and then lose it. For one thing, I didn't know what I wanted to do. I hadn't enough training in the art field—I never would have gotten that first job in California if my father hadn't pulled strings—and I had no other skills. I had just lost a job as a short-order cook and I was low and depressed. Anyway, a guy picked me up at a bar and I went home with him."

"How did you feel about it?"

"Not like the first time. I enjoyed it." He frowns, trying to express his feelings. "It made me feel good, as if I were worth something. Maybe because he thought I was so great. He was an older guy and not too good-looking. It was like I was doing him a favor, and I was something special. Do you know what I mean?"

"I think so." Curiously, I asked, "Did your wife know about it?"

"I didn't tell her. I didn't think she'd understand, and besides, I thought it was wrong. But that didn't stop me. I began looking for homosexual pickups, and I found plenty."

"And was it all casual sex?"

"It was, until about four and a half years ago when we moved here from the Bronx. I met a guy who lived nearby. I had had odd jobs, but at that time neither of us was working, and we ended up seeing each other every day for three and a half months. By then it was a new dimension, a full-fledged homosexual affair. It began to get out of hand. When Ellen would nag me I'd run over to him, and every time he did something I considered faggoty or queer, I'd think, 'Why am I doing this? Why don't I go home to my wife?' Finally he decided I shouldn't be married, that I was really homosexual and hadn't accepted it and my proper place was with him."

"You weren't working during all that time?"

"No. After a long time without work, we decided that I would take care of the house." He gestures at the room. "We agreed I'd stay home and decorate it, at least until I found some kind of work. I really did a hard job. I'd work on the house seven hours straight, painting and building, and then I'd do the cleaning and shopping, then go and spend four or five hours with him. I'd get home after Ellen and give some excuse, like the paint made me sick and I had to take a walk."

"What happened?"

"Well, it got to the point where he thought we should have more than a plain sexual relationship. He'd say, 'We don't have to have sex whenever you come over.' So we wouldn't and I'd leave very frustrated. I began to pick up other guys afterward, but I felt it was wrong. Only I didn't know who I was betraying, him or Ellen. I decided it was time I got some therapy again, but I didn't have enough money. Finally I told him that I couldn't handle our relationship anymore and I needed a few months to get my head together. He said, 'Go ahead, but you'll be back tomorrow.'"

"Were you?"

Frowning, he shakes his head. "It was hard. I was dying to call him the next day, and I kept thinking, should I leave my wife and live with him? I was really questioning what I should do and where I belonged."

Suddenly the baby gives a loud, indignant cry, and David jumps up and runs to the nursery. Roger, who's been reading in the living room, meets us at the door and we all look in at the baby. Her anger evaporates and she breaks into a radiant smile. We walk in and she holds out her arms to me, and we play pick-up-now-go-to-Daddy for a few moments, then David settles her with her bottle and we go back to the bedroom. I try a comfortable-looking rocking chair, painted dark green and stenciled in gold. "I did that myself," David says proudly, settling down on a love seat.

I admire the rocker, then ask, "What came of your questioning?"

"Well, for one thing I got a full-time job driving a cab, and that lasted over a year. Then they raised the rates and people stopped riding in cabs. I was driving in hot traffic all day long without picking anyone up, and I began to get bored with no one to talk to." He's silent for a moment, and I ask, "What happened?"

He shrugs. "I began to get back into the whole homosexual bit."

"But you were still having sex with your wife?"

"Our sex life was always good. But I could have sex with her in the morning, before she went to work, and then I'd spend the day at the baths instead of taking the cab out. It kept up for six or seven months and it got to be quite an emotional drain."

"And physically?"

"Physically, too. I don't know how long it would have gone on, but inevitably I came down with gonorrhea. By the time I found out, Ellen had it, too."

"Did you tell her what happened?"

"I didn't want to, but I felt I had to. I toned it down. I didn't tell her about the baths, but just that I had had some homosexual contacts and I had gonorrhea. That was bad enough. Christ! I never want to go through that again."

"How did she take it?"

"Not well. She was really upset. Poor kid. It was as if her world had come to an end. I felt like a monster—worse, be-

cause at one point she blamed herself, as if she hadn't satisfied me. I was so upset I wanted to kill myself. She cried
and was really sick for a couple of days. She decided we
should split up, and I was terrified at the idea. Then we'd
talk it out, God, how many times we talked things out, over
and over, and then finally she decided she wouldn't leave
me, but that I'd better get myself to a psychiatrist and get
straightened out. She concluded I was basically a good guy
and a good husband, but I was sick."

"But could you afford therapy?"

"Luckily, I found a clinic where you work with a student
therapist at a price we could afford. I went for six months,
and then I realized I had to either give up my wife and
accept homosexuality, or give up men and stay faithful to
Ellen."

"Were you faithful during that time?"

"No. I went to bed with another girl once, a three-way
thing with a guy I knew, and it made me feel so darned
guilty! I seriously considered suicide. I felt it wasn't worth
staying alive. I stayed up all night walking the streets and
trying to get up enough nerve to kill myself."

"But you hadn't felt guilty about sex with men."

"I had, but not like this. I don't know. Maybe if you're
unfaithful, it doesn't matter who it's with, but it didn't
work that way in my head. I felt going to bed with a woman
was the final betrayal to Ellen.

"Finally the therapist asked me, 'Which do you really
want to give up?' and for the first time I faced the fact that
I didn't want to give up any of it, not Ellen or the guys. I
told him, 'I don't want to give up either,' and he said, 'Why
do you feel you have to make a choice?' "

David looks at me challengingly, and I ask, "What about
your wife?"

He nods. "That was it. I asked him that, and he said, 'Why
don't you see if you can get her to deal with the problem.'

I had never thought of it that way, and it seemed kind of unfair, but then I realized that if it was, she could still deal with it. She could leave me. If all she wanted was fidelity, she could find it somewhere else. Why should I leave her? I didn't want to. I loved her too much."

"Did you tell her then?"

"Well, not right away. I didn't have the nerve, to tell the truth. But eventually I got to the point where I could say, 'Look. I'm going to do my best, but I don't think I'll change all that much. Why don't you see a therapist, too? If you want this marriage to work, you're going to have to do some compromising.'"

"Did she agree?"

"Yes, though at first she said we couldn't afford it. Eventually I convinced her that we could and she started going." He runs his fingers through his hair and stands up, pacing the small room restlessly. "That was when my friend Eric came into the picture. He's an old Army buddy married to a girl in Minneapolis. Whenever they could, they'd come East to see us, and once he made a half-pass at Ellen, but nothing came of it. A year later he came East alone, and I knew things had changed. He was just too attentive to Ellen, and finally it came out that he and his wife were splitting up. On that visit he became very involved with Ellen."

"Did she respond?"

"Yes. On his last day here, Ellen asked me, 'What would you think if I went to bed with Eric?' and before I could answer, she began to coax. 'He needs somebody and he's so frustrated. Would it be terribly wrong if I helped him out?'"

"Did it bother you?"

"A little. Not so much that she wanted to go to bed with someone else, but that he was my best friend. But then I realized that I was in no position to preach faithfulness. I had been unfaithful with men, and even with another woman, and she had forgiven me. More than that, I was still continuing my homosexual life and she had accepted that, in fact, she was in therapy trying to work out her acceptance. I thought about it very seriously, and I realized that it needn't mean she loved me any less—hell, I didn't love her less because I fooled around with men. So eventually I said O.K."

"Then Ellen insisted that Eric should think it was my idea. 'He came East just to try and sleep with me,' she said, 'but he can't do it. He's much too fond of you.' And finally I said, 'All right. I'll make it sound like it's my idea.'"

"Did you convince him?"

"Finally. At first he said, 'No, I'm an outsider and I'll only mess up your marriage,' but I insisted that I did my own thing and Ellen should be able to do hers and I'd leave them alone, but he insisted he didn't want that. So finally I came out and said, 'We could all go to bed together.'" He smiles, remembering. "Eric said he'd thought about that, but it wouldn't work because he'd tried to make it with a guy once and the guy didn't turn him on. I said that was his problem. He'd tried it with someone who didn't turn him on. Maybe I would."

"Did you?"

"Sure. We batted it around, and finally we all ended up in bed together because no one wanted to let anyone go. Ellen was dying to go to bed with Eric, but didn't want to exclude me, and Eric wanted me, too. He just had trouble dealing with homosexuality, but it ended up as a very loving fantastic experience. We were three people who had known each other for years, and we did love each other deeply on other levels."

"Is this what you would have liked as a permanent relationship?"

Thoughtfully, he says, "I think so. I fantasized about it at the time, but I don't know if it could have ever worked, if we three could have lived together. Eric's life was out West in Minnesota, and he left the next day, but after he left, my sexual experiences with Ellen became so intense—not only our sexual life, but our life together. I don't know what happened. I don't understand the dynamics of the situation, but it was as if it all came together. It made me very aware of her as a sexual being, and for the first time it seemed as if I could deal with her as a love object in herself instead of having to resort to abstract fantasies because of my homosexuality. Maybe it was because now she knew at first hand what I enjoyed doing with men, but for that whole week after Eric left we were so close in communication and love."

"Did Eric's leaving upset you?"

"No. In a sense it was very good. We didn't have to deal with any embarrassment afterward. We knew we wouldn't see him again, and it's been almost two years and we haven't, even though we've written back and forth."

I ask, "Did the closeness between you and Ellen continue?"

"For a while, but then we were both stunned to discover that Ellen was pregnant."

"Had you wanted a baby?"

"Originally, yes, we wanted one, but when I admitted my homosexuality, we decided we didn't. Still, we never took any precautions because it seemed as if we couldn't conceive. We had both been to doctors and they said nothing was organically wrong. We just forgot about it, and then, wham!"

"This happened after the affair with Eric?"

"Yes, and we thought it might be Eric's child, except that Ellen can tell when she ovulates, and it was almost a month after Eric left that she missed her period. She's very regular."

"So you decided to have the baby?"

"We didn't know what to do, and my therapist and her's both said it had to be our decision, and I didn't know if I could deal with the responsibility of a child. I thought the responsibility of marriage was demanding enough at that time. We did a lot of soul-searching, but eventually it had to be my decision. Ellen just wasn't able to handle the problem. To me, the most important thing was that I genuinely loved Ellen and I wanted to stay married to her, and also that I wanted a baby. I loved kids, and the idea of having one of my own was tremendous. I thought, if the baby is mine I want to have it, and if it's Eric's I still want it. So I told Ellen, 'We're going to have this baby. That's my decision. We're going to have it!' "

"What did she say to that?"

"She was sure it was mine, and now we're both sure because she looks so much like me—her coloring is mine. That makes me feel good, but who her father is doesn't make any difference in terms of how I love her."

"Were you still driving a cab when the baby was born?"

"No. I quit that when Ellen became pregnant. We had saved enough money to have the baby. A friend of mine was opening a bookstore, and he asked me to manage it for him. It sounded like a good solid job, and I accepted."

"Was he a friend in the sexual sense?"

He nods. "Yes. We had been lovers."

"Did Ellen know?"

"Yes. I leveled with her and she accepted it. By now she was able to accept my homosexuality as a part of my nature. That was a big step forward for both of us. It took a tremendous load off my mind. I didn't have to hide and fake excuses to get away, and I stopped worrying constantly about being found out. As for Ellen, she came to understand that my loving men didn't mean I loved her any less. I think that day with Eric made her aware that she, too, could have an affair with someone else and still love me. It also made her aware, seeing Eric and me make love, that homosexuality was nothing to be concerned about."

"Do you honestly think she felt that?"

"Yes, I do. Perhaps it was more than the affair with Eric. It might have been her therapy, but I do know it no longer bothered her. Then, right after the baby was born, I had a big fight with the bookstore owner and I quit. That put me in a hell of a financial position."

"So you were back on the job market."

"I was really upset about losing that job. The fight with the store owner was because I wanted to work for him without being sexually involved, and he wouldn't accept that." He shakes his head, still annoyed at the memory. "I was telling a friend of mine about it, and I said, 'What burns me up is that he didn't want me working for him unless he could have me in bed. It makes me feel like a goddamned whore!' This friend of mine, very casually, said, 'Why don't you try that?' I said, 'What?' and he said, 'Being a whore—a hustler.' So I said, 'Christ, I couldn't. I'm too old and I'm no raving beauty.'" David laughs humorlessly. "He wouldn't buy any of that. He said, 'Every time I'm with you on the street, people turn around and look. You have to face up to the fact that you attract men.' At first I thought he was kidding, but then I realized he was dead serious. He finally told me that he recruited for some New York madams and I could do very well hustling.

"I told him it was crazy, but he didn't let it rest. He kept after me, then and later. As a joke, I told Ellen. I thought she'd blow up, but to my amazement, she said, 'Let's think about it.' I asked her, 'Would you agree to my doing it?' She looked at me for a long time, a funny kind of look as if she were just seeing me, and finally she said, 'You want to do it, don't you?' I just nodded, and she said, 'You've thought about it and you want it. Knowing you, you'll do it no matter what I say, so go ahead. To me it's no different from your sleeping with men as indiscriminately as you do. Look, we've got some kind of honesty going between us. At least, if you go into this you'll be bringing money home.' And that was all she'd say."

"What did you do?"

"I thought it over very carefully then, and I'll admit the idea was very exciting to me. I don't know why, but it seemed as if it was the answer to every fantasy I'd ever had."

"What kind of fantasies?"

He seems embarrassed. "I don't like to go into them, but I've always had fantasies of being used by older, stronger men. Anyway, I told my friend I'd go along with it, and he sent me to a couple of clients, or rather, he sent me to a madam who sent me out."

Confused, I ask, "By madam do you mean a woman?"

David laughs. "Oh, no. They were men, and I hustled for men."

"Well, how did it work?"

"It was all done by telephone. I had a second phone put in, and the madams would call me when they had a client."

"How much of a cut do they take?"

"That varies. With a lot of them, on a thirty-dollar call, I'd get twenty and they'd take a ten-dollar cut."

"Where do you go?"

"Sometimes it's to a hotel room, or to someone's apartment."

"What are your clients like?"

David considers. "I don't think I can put them into any general category. Some are so advanced in their sexual appetites that they need constant new stimuli. They've done everything you can do in bed, and they want freakier things all the time. Some of it is very bizarre activity that really goes beyond the sexual. It's a whole different area, and they're at the point where they know they'll have to pay to get it."

"And you're able to furnish them with it?"

David leans back and hooks his thumbs in his belt. "Look, I've come to think of myself as a glass pitcher. Pour red liquid into me and I'm red. Pour in blue and I'm blue. I've gotten into things I wouldn't go looking for, nor do I care if I ever do them again. But when they came up, I did them as a job. I was paid and I did it."

There's a knock on the door and Roger pokes his head in. "She asleep now, David. I have an errand to run, but I'll be back in half an hour. O.K.?"

"Sure. Just leave the door open."

When Roger leaves, I ask David, "Are you saying you wouldn't get a kick out of any of this without being paid?"

He shrugs. "I'll try anything once, but when I'm looking for sex for myself I try to find someone to connect with, to communicate with. If I can respond to somebody's voice or eyes, I don't care too much what we do in bed."

"But for pay you'll do anything?"

He hesitates. "No, not really. I've turned down some of the freakier things."

"Does that happen often?"

"No. Look, I hear a lot about men hustling because their self-respect is low and this is a way of humiliating themselves, but I don't feel that. Most people who pay for sex do it because they want to pay. It seems to alleviate their guilt. Anyway, whatever the reason, I did well."

"Do you mean financially?"

"Yes. I was absolutely overwhelmed. The first week I made over three hundred and ninety-five dollars. For someone who rarely made more than sixty dollars a week, that was incredible."

"How many customers would you have a day?"

"That week I worked hard. I was seeing three, four, maybe five men a day. Of course, I didn't make that kind of money again. I'd have run myself ragged if I kept up that pace. Now it's cooled down considerably. Instead of relying

on the madams, I advertise in some of the X-rated magazines."

"Why did you stop using the madams?"

"I didn't really stop. They still call me occasionally, but
you have to realize I've been in the business for two years
now, and these madams have a regular clientele. A lot of
the men who deal with hustlers keep wanting something
new. They want every new boy in town. I'm in demand for
three, four, even five times, and that's good for this racket.
Eventually they get tired of me." He's thoughtful for a
moment, then sighs. "It makes me think that maybe my
hustling days are almost over. I'm getting too old for it
anyway. In general, Ellen and I seem to be in for a period
of change. In the past year my wife and I have started
having threesomes quite often. Sometimes I run into customers who like girls, too, so I bring them home, if Ellen
agrees. Now she's starting to enjoy threesomes. She's at the
point where once she lets her hair down, she enjoys it, and
she's learning a lot of things about herself and her own
sexuality. She's still at a point where she doesn't really deal
with it on an intellectual level. If she's talked into it, she
enjoys it. It's like being seduced and liking it afterward.
She hasn't yet brought anyone home herself, though she's
had fantasies about it."

"Has she had any lesbian experiences?"

"No, though recently she's begun to realize that she
finds women attractive. She just never opened her mind to
it before."

"But do you think that's something you could approach
on an intellectual level?"

"Why not? Anybody can function on a homosexual level
if their mind is there. If their mind never gets to that level,
they can't. I mean, if a thing is always repulsive to you, you
won't get into it. Before I had overt homosexual experiences,
the idea repelled me. I found it offensive."

"And now?"

"Now I figure, if the male body is attractive to a woman, why shouldn't it be attractive to me? Should I be repelled by a body like mine? At one time, my wife accepted the idea that I'd go to bed with men, but she felt that seeing it would disturb her. Now that she's been involved with it and realizes that it can be loving and affectionate, she feels differently. She had society's idea that we're all weirdos and freaks, but now she knows we're people. And people communicate with people and make love to them, men or women."

"But do you find none of it disturbing or abnormal?"

"Sure. There are certain things I just can't see or want or understand."

"But doesn't it get boring?"

He nods thoughfully. "I guess it does. But I've been very involved with other things. I've been approached to speak to gay groups. One asked me to speak about hustling. They had never interviewed a hustler before. Then I decided to do it up right. I wore a tux and I asked Ellen to come along and wear her Victorian gown." He gestures at the dress form with the elaborate red-velvet gown. "I didn't lie to them and say I'd become very successful, but the tux and gown were lies to produce the image I wanted to project, and it worked. It was a very successful evening. I was accepted as a sort of sex symbol, even a superstar type. I got a big ego trip out of that." He sighs. "I feel very healthy and happy and very valid as a human being, and that's since I've come out and accepted my needs and started dealing with them. My marriage hasn't fallen apart, and only positive things have happened."

"And you've been active politically."

"Look at this." He gets me a colored 8 by 10 photograph of himself in a plaid suit and boater, Ellen in a long, turn-of-the-century street dress, and the baby in the elaborately decorated carriage. "That was taken in Central Park when we marched in the last Gay Liberation parade. I asked Ellen to come because I told her I'd appreciate having her. She was part of my thing, and she thought about it and finally decided to dress up and take the baby in her carriage. We marched in the parade and were interviewed, and God knows how many pictures of the baby were taken!"

"Did the publicity interfere with Ellen's job in any way?"

"Not at all. As a matter of fact, she told most of the girls in the office about it. They like me. I'm a sex symbol to them. Hell, their husbands are businessmen or engineers, and me, I make my living with sex. They think it's great."

"What about her boss?"

"He doesn't know and probably won't find out, but it doesn't bother Ellen. She's a very skilled secretary and can find a job anywhere at any time."

"Do your parents know anything about your life?"

"No, they don't. They know I'm married and they've seen pictures of the baby. That's enough for them." His voice hardens. "Nothing I could do would ever please my father or make him think I was a man, so why the hell should I try? That one visit home with Ellen opened my eyes. My mother was a bitch to her. Well, I don't need that. I don't need my family, and I don't really want them. They're a continent away and that suits me fine!"

"And Ellen's parents?"

"They're in the Midwest and we rarely see them. They have no idea about us, though I suppose someday they'll know." He leans forward intently. "I don't really like all this closet stuff. After the gay parade our consciousness was raised. Ellen and I are working on a group for other gay couples, or bisexual couples. So many people came up to us at the parade and said, 'Look, I'm gay and my wife doesn't know,' or 'She knows, but she figures it's my thing.' Ellen and I have been trying to raise other people's consciousness."

"Are your neighbors aware of all this?"

"Ah, I think they suspect. They're acquaintances, but not close friends. We baby-sit back and forth, and I bullshit with the husband and the wife comes up and talks to Ellen, but they're not intimately involved with my personal life. It's not as if I'm going to go down and say, 'Hey! I'm bisexual. What are you?' Anyway, I don't know if they could deal with it if they knew for sure."

"What will you tell your daughter when she grows up?"

"She'll grow up knowing that this is the way things are done in our family, and she'll never have to be told anything." He frowns. "She won't be taught there's anything wrong with it, or bizarre. If for any reason her schoolmates find out and tease her, well, children are attacked on many levels." His face, knotted in anxiety, belies his easy words. "If a child is secure in her own environment, she can deal with it."

As I get ready to leave, I notice that there are very few books in the room outside of the ones there for decoration. "Do you or Ellen read much?" I ask.

"Ellen reads a little and I'm starting to. I've become very political lately, now that my own house is cleaned up. I know myself better, and I can start projecting ideas and theories and doing constructive things."

I take one last look at the baby, sleeping on her stomach with her fist against her mouth, and I walk toward the subway, down the suburban, tree-lined streets, feeling very sad and distressed, unable to get the baby's image out of my mind.

One's first reaction to reading about David and Ellen might be that he has a really deep-seated problem and is totally "abnormal." Again we have to be careful not to equate something "way out" and different with something "abnormal." It is certainly true that being a hustler puts David in an infinitesimally small minority, but does that make him abnormal? I do not believe so. We must look at the motivation if we are to get any insight into the meaning of his actions and if we are going to attempt to look into a crystal ball to find his future.

Underneath David's hustling activities lies a simple truth. He got into it as an easy way out of not being able to cope with the economic necessities of life. As the reader will recall, he got really involved in it when he was in desperate financial straits and didn't know where to turn. A friend was the one who suggested this way of life. We must keep in mind that David never earned much money and in the first week he earned $395, which was an absolute fortune to him, never having earned more than $60 in any one week previously.

At this point one is seriously tempted to question why he didn't find some other way of making money—to ask what were the peculiar motivations that led him to choose this means of gaining a livelihood. We may be complicating things unnecessarily by making the assumption that if one chooses a deviant approach to economic problems, there must exist complicated unconscious processes that are different from those of the average person. This does not have to be true.

How many men do we know who are in the jobs they are in because they truly like them? How many men made a conscious choice of their life's work? In the majority of cases I think we would discover that men drift into their work through some sort of accident. They know someone who can get them a job when their schooling is finished, whether it be at the high-school level or the college level. After the passage of time, this earlier accident is forgotten. I think it safe to say that if David had not found himself out of a job, and had not run into a man who suggested this way out, he would never have become involved in the life of a hustler.

In spite of his homosexual activities, he does not seem to be functioning on any dynamic homosexual level. He enjoys his sexual relations with his wife. He really does not find himself in the grips of a constant "need" for men.

David senses his days as a hustler may be coming to an end because of his age and his connections with the madams. I believe this will cause a serious problem for him —not because of his sexual drive, but for quite another reason. He will face what I call re-entry problems. He has been making easy money and working whenever he pleases at whatever rate he pleases. When he has to go back to work, he may well be unable to face the demands of a lower-paying job. He has no training or special talents that would lead him to either a good or a well-paying job.

I have encountered the same problem with men who have become drug dealers. They make easy money with little work and find it almost impossible to handle a regular steady job. Often the person never adjusts and is permanently lost as a productive member of society. David runs a high risk of this.

We cannot leave out of consideration here David's relationship to his father. David describes him as a man who never listened to him and who liked to push people around. This extended to David when he worked in the same office as his father. Also he had his first homosexual experience right after he severed his work relationship with his father. One is tempted to connect these two occurrences in a causal manner, but it is not necessary to see a causal relationship between two events simply because they happen next to each other in time. In this case, I believe the important thing was the fact that this first man listened to David and seemed truly interested in him. "He wanted to hear about all the things I wanted to talk about and never could." This experience of being listened to by a homosexual could easily have led David into looking for other such experiences. It would not be easy to say which he would be looking for—homosexuality or being listened to.

In looking at his first sexual experience with a woman, David said, "It was awful." In the beginning, sexual experience with both men and women was fraught with trauma and caused him to be very upset. I would say David is not into any type of sex on an emotional level. Although he participates in all types of sexual activity with either sex, it is almost entirely on a superficial level. There does not seem to be any deep drive one way or the other.

Along this line, one would have to question his willingness to use his wife as a prostitute from time to time. There are many men who have the fantasy of seeing their wives in bed making love to another man or to a woman, but very few would be willing to turn their wives into prostitutes even for one evening.

We do not have any information from Ellen herself about her feelings, but from my experience with women patients over the past thirty years, I would have serious doubts about her being so accepting of his bisexual life. Men have a way of thinking that their wives are accepting something when in reality they have, at the best, a begrudging tolerance.

There is also another broader question highlighted in the life of this couple. Is it possible to love two people at the same time? David thinks so: "My loving men didn't mean I loved her any less." We do not know what Ellen thinks. When a man goes to bed with a woman who is not his wife, he will often tell her he is in love with her, and our automatic assumption is that he is kidding himself. Does this have to be so? Could it be possible to love two people at the same time?

I think we have to consider seriously the possibility that

this can be true. Like so many other ideas, it may depend on how we define the word "love." Poets and writers throughout the centuries have tried to define this word, but it always has a way of squirming out of any definition we attempt to pin on it. A man loves his wife, his children, his dog. I think it safe to say these are different types of love. Love does not have to be mutually exclusive. Most men have little or no problem in loving their mothers and their wives at the same time. They know in their hearts that they are different kinds of love. Perhaps we can think of bisexuality in the same light.

If we equate sex with love, then we are forced to look upon bisexuality as an unresolved conflict in each and every case. It might be possible for some people to honestly regard sex as merely a game to be played with someone one enjoys and completely reserve the feelings of love for other levels. Most married couples have experienced a lessening of the sexual drive for their partners after they have been married for a number of years. They have also experienced a deepening of what they call "love" for their partners. The true bisexual may have successfully accomplished this division in another way.

In the case of David, our safest conclusion is that his bisexual activities are a result of his economic problems combined with those brought about by his father. He is not a true bisexual even though his behavior is on that level. When and if he finds a good job, he will most likely give up being a hustler. He is functioning at a superficial emotional level, since he is not able to relate deeply to either sex.

6

Jean

I am to meet Jean where she works, an elegant dress shop on upper Madison Avenue. The store is glass and chrome and suede, the customers outnumbered by slim young sales-women. Jean herself is tall, slim, and quite beautiful, her blonde hair falling down her back, her features as clearly cut as a cameo. She is French, but there is an English fresh-ness to her complexion. She wears a white T-shirt and blue velvet slacks with a little medallion around her neck.

Jean shows me two armchairs upholstered in brown suede, but I look around uncertainly. "Is there some place more quiet or private?"

She takes me to a dressing room in the rear and brings in a chair for me while she perches on a three-legged wooden stool. We are only a few feet apart, and I am almost uncomfortably aware of her. She smiles, and her teeth are small and even. I ask, "How long have you been bisexual?"

"Oh, for four or five years." She speaks English well, but there is a strong and charming French accent.

"And before that?"

A little Gallic shrug. "I was only heterosexual."

"What changed you?"

"Changed?" She considers a moment. "Awakened, perhaps. I have always been interested in women. When I was just a child I would look at women in the street. I was never turned on by men, only by women." She laughs. "I would come out of a movie when I was a child and I would remember the women in the picture, their dresses, their bodies— the men were shadows. But, you know, living in Europe, in Paris with a very strict family, you just don't think like that. I never allowed myself to."

"But you did change."

"Oh, yes. When I came to New York. I met a woman who was a lesbian, and we became very good friends, and it was she who made me come out. She initiated me, and then I was able to start my own homosexual life."

Puzzled, I ask, "Homosexual? You mean bisexual."

"Oh, no. I was, for a year and a half, totally homosexual. I absolutely didn't go out with men. I didn't want to see men on a sexual level."

"But you're not homosexual now?"

"I changed. After a while I began to be more together about it. I began to see people as people, not men or women —a human being first, a sexual partner second—and I came back to men."

"But not to heterosexuality?"

She shakes her head, then brushes her hair back from her forehead, and the gesture is disturbingly feminine. I am intensely aware of her close presence in the small room, and I am aware, too, that she is wearing no scent. "It doesn't matter to me whether I have a man or a woman in bed with me. To me the difference is slight, and yet—I would rather be with a woman."

"You mean if you had your preference?"

"Right."

"Have you always felt that way?"

"Unconsciously I have, but I never allowed myself to admit it, to come out in the open and say, 'I would prefer a woman.'"

"Your first sexual experience was with a man?"

She nods.

"When was that?"

"When I was sixteen." Again the smile, but almost sad now. "I was not raped, but it was close. I was forced. I don't think it affected me very deeply, I mean, it didn't leave any unconscious marks on me. In fact, I felt very proud about it afterward."

"In what way, proud?"

"I realized that I was a woman. I was only sixteen, but I had turned someone on. I had aroused something in a man so strong that he had to force me into sex in order to satisfy it. I had to be quite a woman to do that!"

"How did it happen?"

"I was hitchhiking the night before, and he picked me up and took me right to my door. He was very nice, good-looking and much older. He behaved himself so well, maybe I was a little disappointed. He invited me to a party the next night, and I said, 'Sure.'" She moves a bit uncomfortably and her forehead wrinkles. There is a tension about her that is at odds with her calm voice. "We had a great evening, and then he drove me to a quiet place and raped me—or forced me. It was not a good start for sex."

"Did you have trouble having sex with men after that?"

She looks appalled. "Oh, never! I have never had trouble sexually. Perhaps I have unconscious bad memories of that incident, but I don't think so. When I talk about it, even now, I just don't care. I never cared about it. I never thought of it or had bad dreams about it."

I wonder at that. She seems too vehement, too intent on

convincing herself as well as me, but her voice is calm. I go back to an earlier theme. "You say that women turn you on. Can you react to a man's lovemaking?"

"Oh, yes. I am turned on by some men, but by more women. Let's say I meet ten men, maybe one will turn me on. But if I meet ten women, there would be five I was turned on by."

"Did you have many affairs with men before you came to America?"

"Yes, and I still have many affairs, even now."

"After your period of homosexuality, did you go back to men?"

"Yes, but mostly to bisexual men."

"Why?"

She smiles a bit mischievously. "Bisexual men are better lovers." She waits for a moment, and when I don't challenge this, she says, "Besides, the men who know that I am bisexual are also bisexual."

"Since this happened, have you even been with a man who doesn't know?"

"I don't think I have. Or if I have been, I didn't know it."

"Why do you think it's better if a man knows you are bisexual?"

"His knowing doesn't make it better. It's just—well, perhaps it's just a coincidence, but all the men I have slept with recently are bisexual. I never said, 'Listen. I'm a bisexual.' But it always came out. They always knew."

"Do you feel that making love to a bisexual man is different from making love to a heterosexual man?"

"Oh yes!" She is very definite.

"But why? What's the difference?"

She looks up with a smile and spreads her hands in an opening gesture, as if she would encompass the whole matter in her arms. "A bisexual man is much more aware of my sensitivity. He is better at all the preliminary lovemaking. Perhaps it's because he's not as selfish as a heterosexual man."

I start to protest, but she stops me. "No, wait. Maybe I'm generalizing, because not all heterosexual men are selfish. But—how do I say it?" She shrugs disarmingly. "Most of them don't know what a woman wants, that a woman can be made love to for over an hour. They are always concerned with their own performance. They are forever asking, 'Did I do it right? Did you come yet?' As if it were a task to be accomplished. They cannot relax into lovemaking, and I—I always feel pressured to respond. I begin to feel that I am not living up to what they want, that I am lacking in response. A bisexual man is more aware of what a woman wants. Having sex with a bisexual man is usually more—well, positive."

She pauses, smiling at me with a little challenge, waiting for me to protest. Instead, I say, "Tell me more about what a bisexual man is."

"Ah. First of all he is more sensitive. He is more romantic in his relationships. But this is also true of homosexual men. I have had homosexual lovers." There is a wicked glint in her eye. "Are you surprised?"

"A little, perhaps, that you can differentiate."

"Oh, I can. You know, homosexual men and bisexual men will talk to me about their affairs with other men, and it's much like listening to a woman. They will discuss everything. What it's like to be weak and to love someone, to be all upset because he didn't call the night before. I have rarely heard heterosexual men talk like that about women. It would destroy them, most of them. Their pride wouldn't allow it, their masculine pride."

"Are you saying that bisexual men have more feminine qualities than straight men?"

She nods eagerly. "That's just it. Yes, definitely. But it's more than that. They overcome the barriers that society has put up. They don't believe that men should not show emotion and sensitivity."

"Is that what you like in men?"

She hesitates, leaning back against the wall of the fitting room. "I think I really prefer a balance in between. But what I want in a man is someone who sees life the way I do."

"I'm not sure I understand that."

"If I'm with a straight man and I meet a woman on the street I may turn on to her. He can't take that, that I might like a woman better than I like him. It destroys his male pride. A bisexual man isn't concerned about that pride."

"You mean your bisexuality is a threat to straight men?"

"Oh, definitely, definitely. Sometimes I'll go to a bar, or to a party with a straight friend—I have a few, you know—and we'll both look at the same girl, and I'll say, 'I want her,' and they say, 'No! I want her,' and they get very up tight. They're afraid I'll get her before they do, and that would mean they were less of a man. I don't understand that, especially when they tell me they're trying to be very free and open. They are afraid, and jealous."

"Do you find less jealousy among bisexual men?"

"Yes, bisexual men are less jealous, and homosexual men have more jealousy, but they are jealous of other men."

"Have you often been in a relationship with three people?"

"Several times, usually with another woman and a man, but often with two men."

"Two bisexual men?"

"Yes." She grimaces slightly. "But I don't enjoy that at all, two men making love to each other."

"Why is that?"

"I don't know why." She teeters on the stool and tilts her head back to look up at me, as if trying to put a few extra feet between us. "I just don't appreciate male homosexuality."

"You don't like to see it?"

"I think it's disgusting," she says quickly, and then catches herself. She has taken an attitude out of line with her freethinking, and she realizes it. "Maybe not disgusting, but it just turns me off."

"But you don't mind two women making love."

"Oh, definitely not." She straightens up and smiles.

"Do you think that's fair?"

She pouts. "Of course it's not." Implied here is, allow me to be unreasonable. Then, as if to explain, she says, "I don't think another man would attract me if I were a man. I think—I can't be positive."

"Yet as a bisexual woman you say your are attracted by a man."

"Yes, but if I were a man, another man would not attract me. Another woman would." Impatient at my denseness, she spreads her hands. "I just don't understand male homosexuality."

Something in my expression bothers her. "I shouldn't say things like this. I don't understand it, and I can't explain why I react the way I do, but the first time I saw two men together it repulsed me. I couldn't look at it. Maybe because I wasn't the center of attention, because I couldn't participate . . ."

I see that the question upsets her, and I move away from it. "Do you find a lot of bisexuality in the city?"

She nods, still a little ruffled.

"How about other cities?"

Brusquely, she says, "I don't know other cities."

"Has most of your bisexual life been here?"

"Yes. When I leave the city I go with friends who are either bisexual or homosexual, and we visit other friends who are the same way. But anywhere else it just isn't as open as it is here."

"Where in New York do you find it?"

She throws back her head and laughs. "Where don't I find

it? In the store here I am picked up by a customer at least once a week. If I like them I can let them know that I'm available. Just with a look." She looks at me with subtle difference in her glance, an appraising look that disturbs me without my knowing why. Then she laughs. "I have to pretend with a man, but it comes naturally with a woman. I drop a phrase or two to show them I'm open and not afraid—you can be sure they'll call me the week after."

I feel that I must challenge her. "How do you know they're not lesbians?"

"I know because I've met them." She seems to lose interest in the subject. "Maybe three-quarters are bisexual."

I move back to an earlier question. "You say you don't like to see two men making love, but in a relationship with a bisexual man you knew he had affairs with other men."

"Of course, whenever he wanted to. But I never participated."

"Would he participate when you were with another woman?"

"It would depend on the woman I was with. If I have a relationship with a bisexual woman, a man can come in. That's fine—if she agrees to it. I would never force the issue. I'd say, 'I have this friend of mine who's very nice. What do you think?' And she would say yes or no. But if I'm involved with a true homosexual woman, I would never even ask the question. I'd know the answer."

"Do you feel that sex with a woman is as satisfying as with a man?"

Raising one eyebrow, Jean says, "More!"

"But the men you go with are experienced. Surely they can make love as well as women."

She pushes her lower lip forward and considers. "Maybe I'm unlucky, but of all the men I've had, and there have been quite a few, I have met only, say, ten who knew what they were doing. A woman, even if she has never been

with another woman, knows right away." Seeing my doubtful look, she leans forward intently. "There's no doubt about
it. If you're a woman you know what you want done to
yourself, and what to do to another woman. Most women
want the same thing."

I am still unconvinced. "But surely you can show a man
what to do."

"Of course I show them, and I always think I'm giving
them a gift. But so few have the patience and understanding."

"Does the physical body of a man have any appeal to
you?"

"Yes." She smooths the velvet of her pants along her
thighs. "I enjoy making love to a man. I definitely enjoy
that."

I hear the distinction. "What about him making love to
you?"

Her eyes are downcast, considering the long, smooth
line of her own legs. "A man making love to me is just not
as successful as if it were a woman. Perhaps I am more open
with a woman."

"Do you live with a man or a woman usually."

She looks up at me, her eyes clear and disarming, their
light blue reflecting the blue of her pants. "I am living
alone—now. I lived with a woman for three years, but since
then I haven't found anyone I want to settle with."

"Do your parents know you are bisexual?"

She laughs at that, but I catch a moment of dismay. "No
way!"

"Would they mind?"

"Mind? They are European, which means they are very
narrow-minded."

"Do your friends know, your friends here?"

"Oh, yes, all my friends know."

"And do they accept it?"

"If they don't that's too bad. My friends accept me the way I am or not at all. I have a lot of friends here and I'm very happy about what I am." She leans back against the wall and folds her arms across her chest. "If it comes up and people talk about bisexuality, I won't play a hypocrite's role. If they ask have I been trying it, I say yes. If they don't like that, I don't want them around me."

"You have no conflict about it?"

"None. Never! I have never felt conflict or guilt about sex. It just seems something natural, a natural part of life."

"What was your father like?"

She uncrosses her arms and sits up a bit. "Tender and extremely intelligent and affectionate. He cared so for us, for me and my sister. I feel very good about him." She hesitates. "It was hard to talk to him when I was younger, but not when I was older." She puts her elbow on her knee and leans her chin on her fist. "He always disliked seeing me with boys. Once he caught me kissing one, and he didn't talk to me for weeks. But that was because he was hurt," she adds quickly.

"Hurt?"

"To think I would be that easy. He was afraid I would take up with men who weren't good enough for me, and most of them weren't. I could bring girl friends home and he'd always be nice to them. That wasn't bad because now I could even go back home with a woman lover and she could sleep in my bed and my parents would accept it." She leans back chewing her lip. "Sometimes I wonder, am I going with women to please my father?" She laughs a bit sadly. "Now he's writing me letters all the time, sentimental stuff, like I should think about getting married and settling down."

"And your mother?"

Her smile softens. "My mother was the first woman I loved. I adore her. I used to sit on her lap, kissing and touching her for hours, even in my teens. She would never put me down for it, or reproach me. I think she sensed there was more than affection—there was some sexual love there."

"When did you start dating boys?"

"I was fourteen. In Europe such things happen later than in the States."

"And you had no experience with other women until you came here?"

"Yes, well, I never met anyone." She hesitates, chewing her lip. "When I was sixteen I had an affair with a much older man, he was forty, and in bed he once asked me, 'Have you ever slept with a woman?' I was shocked and said, 'No! Of course not!' But then he started to tell me how nice it would be, that a woman would really know my body and what I liked, and I started thinking about what he said, then and after I left him, and back in Paris I tried looking for another woman, but I was too bashful then to just approach a straight girl because I didn't even know what to do. I had read about homosexuality, but in Paris it was so underground I just didn't know where to go to find it— not until I came here."

"But after your period with homosexuality you went back to men."

She lifts her arm to brush her hair back and in the cramped fitting room she brushes against me. She smiles in a quick apology, but I have a feeling the contact is deliberate. "It was very difficult, going back to men. The sex was strange. The first time I was very tense."

"Why?"

She shakes her head. "It was peculiar to feel big hands on my body, and the rough skin of a man, but still—I really wanted him as a man."

"Why?"

She moves uncomfortably. "Perhaps I should say as a person. I liked him first as a person, then as a man, and I didn't realize it would be so strange."

"Was it a long affair?"

"It was a very strange affair. He understood me, all about me very quickly, and for a while we were lovers, but somehow he sensed that as a lover I would drop him after a month or so. It was very intense in the beginning, but he knew, before I did, that it wouldn't last, so after two weeks he said to me, 'Jean, I know what you are and I want to be your friend, and I don't want to ruin that friendship with sex. Let's be friends instead of lovers.' So we became very, very close friends, and we still are."

"Was he bisexual?"

"No, he was straight. He was." She grins wickedly. "Since we met he has had two homosexual affairs."

"Why did he do that?"

Seriously, she says, "To give himself strength. When he came to know me and saw that I didn't have any problems, just because I was bisexual, he wanted to try it himself." I must look doubtful, for she continues very earnestly, "I feel I am very free sexually. The straight women I know have hang-ups that I don't have. To them it would seem very crude to go down on a man."

"Not to all straight women," I protest.

She brushes this aside. "To most. They don't believe it's nice, or proper, or fun. God, how can you have sex if you're stopped by such worries? When I am in bed with someone I would do anything to make him happy."

"But for that matter, how many men will go down on a woman?"

She draws herself up a little. "Every man always went down on me!"

"Yet even with that, you find their lovemaking not as knowledgeable as women's?"

"Well!" She throws her arms up. "Even if they do it, they don't always know how to do it. Men should be taught this in school!"

Anger flatters her. I smile, and she catches it and laughs. "All right, but I am very serious about this."

Changing the subject, I ask, "How do you dress? For men or women?"

"For me. I wear what I like. Sometimes, like when I was going through my homosexual phase, I would dress very butch, men's suits. But anyway, I never wear dresses. I always wear pants."

There is nothing remotely butch about the blue velvet pants. They are elegant and feminine, and the T-shirt is revealing. "Why do you always wear pants?"

Without meaning it, she offers, "Maybe I don't like my legs." At my disbelieving look, she laughs. "It's just that I'm more comfortable in pants, not that they're mannish—once I used to be very conscious of how I dressed, when I was going to all the gay bars. Everyone thinks I'm feminine, you know, I'm pretty and have long blonde hair. They'd immediately figure I was a passive type, and I'm not. When I was cruised in a bar, I wanted them to be sure to see what I was. By wearing men's clothes I was saying, 'This is what I am.' I think that's the only time I ever tried a role."

"Are you ever passive in a relationship with a woman?"

"Usually we don't play parts. We just complement each other. You know, butch-femme role-playing is dying out."

"And with men?"

Her face takes on a slightly sulky look. "I don't want to, but I always end up being the aggressor. What I'd like is a man who would dominate me, but I find very few."

"I think it would be easy to find a man to dominate you, but could such a man measure up to your standards of lovemaking?"

She looks at me sharply to see if I'm teasing. Then, satisfied, she shrugs. "I've met one man who can. He dominates me and knows how to make love, but he seldom comes to New York. I see him maybe four times a year, and he never tells me he missed me, or even that he cares for me, and yet on the phone we talk like old friends, and when he is with me the sex between us is mad, fantastic."

"Is he married?"

"No, he's very young."

"And you think his aggressiveness is what turns you on?"

"That, and the fact that he says so little; there's so much mystery about him." She leans forward intently, her hand touching my arm. "Most men begin to hand me the same bullshit after a week. 'I love you. You're so great. I'll do anything you want.' I really feel that I can demand anything and they'll give it to me."

I am conscious of her hand against my arm. "You don't want that?"

"No, I don't. That's why I like a relationship with a woman. I can't fool another woman, and she can't fool me. I know the tricks she's going to use and she knows if I'm lying or sincere."

I cross my arms, and Jean's hand drops away. You're saying that you can manipulate a man, and you can't manipulate a woman."

"Yes. I don't want to be able to walk over a man. When I begin to manipulate them I want them to smack me in the face and say, 'Stop it.' Maybe it's American men. A European man wouldn't let me get away with it." She considers a moment. "Or maybe it's just that American women are so dominant. They'll say to their husbands, 'Don't buy that shirt, but this one,' and the dummy does!"

"The women's liberation groups have all attacked this dominating quality but you say you like it."

"Well, I feel men are strong in certain areas and women in others, but I find that bisexual men are more equal."

"But isn't that a contradiction? You say you like a man who will dominate you, that you like bisexual men, but bisexual men are less prone to be aggressive, to try to dominate."

"There's no contradiction. A bisexual man won't let me get away with things I get away with with a straight man.

There's no fighting for dominance. We have a totally different relationship. It's quiet, free, and understanding. There is no game-playing."

"Do you know why?"

She is quiet for a long time, chewing the end of her thumbnail, then, slowly, she says, "Perhaps because bisexual men don't have such an ego problem. They don't have to prove themselves."

"Are the bisexual men you know truly bisexual, or are they homosexual men who sleep with women?"

She answers very quickly, to my surprise. "No. Most of the men I sleep with are truly bisexual. I know because I have a lot of homosexual men friends. There are two who are truly homosexual but have slept with me. One has been homosexual for ten years—he's forty-eight—and I'm the only woman he's slept with. We've been together four or five times, more for tenderness than anything else."

For a moment she seems lost in the memory of the affair, then she shakes her head and her voice becomes a bit harder. "The thing I get angry about is that all of a sudden bisexuality is in, and a lot of people are calling themselves bisexual when they really aren't. If it's in to have group sex, they have group sex. If it's in to be bisexual, they're bisexual."

Slowly, I say, "Perhaps a lot of people who are truly bisexual are just now finding some justification for it. Perhaps they're coming out of the closet."

She laughs at that and looks at me closely. "Well? It should be good for us, even if it only makes more people available."

"Do you ever think of marriage or children?"

She is wearing a ring with a stone on her left hand, and now she twists it around so only the band shows. Holding it up, she considers it. "No. Oh, I wouldn't say it will never happen. How can I be positive? But I don't want it, at least now. I can't see myself with one man. When I think of the future I think of a career. I would like to fall madly in love with a woman and maybe do something in business together."

"Do you think it would be easier to make a life with a woman?"

She turns the ring back with a sigh. "It would be a totally different life."

"But isn't it possible to have a new type of marriage with a bisexual man—and still have a family?"

Doubtfully, she says, "Yes. But would it be good for our children? Have I the right to impose my lifestyle on anyone else? If they grew up in that kind of atmosphere, you know, seeing me with a woman lover, their father with a man lover—I mean, for children to understand . . ."

"You think it would disturb them?"

"It's not so much that. I don't feel it would be right for me to put this on them when they were children. Let them discover it for themselves. If they want to take that path, let them take it."

Carefully, I ask, "Do you feel society has the right to dictate to children in terms of love: you must love the other sex, not your own?"

"No, but I wouldn't put children there right away. I want them to make a choice."

"But do any of us have the choice if the society tells us what is right and wrong?"

She frowns at me for a moment, then abruptly smiles. "Maybe I'm just too young, and I don't want children yet." She lifts both her hands to push her hair back. "If I ever fall madly in love with a man who is straight, which I doubt, I would think of children. I could be very faithful if I made up my mind to stay with one man."

"Have you ever been that faithful?"

"Oh, yes, once for two years and once for three years. I

may have looked or flirted, but I never did anything. I didn't want to."

"Do you prefer long relationships?"

She looks at me calculatingly. "Right now I would like a long-term relationship." She hesitates. "With a bisexual man who will leave me all the freedom I want, but I don't know. If we truly loved each other, could we accept the other running around? Intellectually I could, but my emotions wouldn't. I'm afraid that where there's love there's always jealousy."

Afterward we walk to the store entrance together, and Jean lets me out on Madison Avenue. "It is really," she says in farewell, "a wonderful city for a bisexual."

Jean is a woman—of that there is no doubt. We are not talking about a lesbian in the popular sense of the word. She is no man-hater, she has not competed in the world of women for the attention of men and lost. The wiles of women used in sexual games are at her disposal, and she uses them at will. When she walks down the street, men stop and stare. Her dress is feminine in a way French women uniquely possess. There are no vibrations of hostility emanating from her personality—she is vibrant and electric in her every action and movement. She reminds me of a well-groomed, self-possessed cat moving confidently through a forest of people, interacting with whomever she chooses.

There is some risk of being thought a male chauvinist if I speak of a feminine way of thinking, but with Jean I must say that she thinks in a manner we have been culturally conditioned to associate with women. She mixes guile with directness that keeps one constantly off balance. One gets the sense that he is being played with, but for no negative ulterior motive. It all seems a game in which one is a willing player and no one wins or loses. This is all accomplished without a sense of being threatened. Her mind is quick and jumps from one topic to another, like quicksilver on a marble tabletop. In our culture, the feminine mind is supposed to be governed more by emotions than logic. One has the distinct impression that Jean's major motivation springs from her feelings rather than her mind. If the two were to clash, it would be her logic that would lose the battle.

In any attempt to understand the behavior of a person, it is necessary to take a detailed look into his past history. We are all the sum total of our past. It would not be unlikely to find that a person who has an abiding fear of dogs had been badly frightened by a dog as a child. Unfortunately, in attempting to explain the present-day behavior of a particular person, it is not usually possible to trace the reason for the behavior back to a single event, whether it be in his childhood or in the past few months. A particular type of behavior is usually accounted for by many reasons, like a river formed by numerous little mountain streams running together. It is not really possible to know all the events in a person's life that may have played a part in making him behave as he does. All we can do is take the few known events and statements and try our best to see if they throw some light on that person's present behavior. Often we end up with only an educated guess about what causes a person to act as he does in any given set of circumstances.

We know a few things about Jean's background that may help us understand her present-day behavior. Her father was an important figure in her life, especially in reference to forming her sexual attitudes. I would say he was very straightlaced and puritanical. During her early teen-age years Jean's father would not only talk to her if she kissed a boy but would fly into a rage, telling her she was a tramp and no good. In effect, he withdrew his approval if she had any physical contact with boys. It went further in that he gave Jean the very specific feeling that there was no boy good enough for her. His attitude was strong enough and expressed vehemently enough to set up various patterns of behavior toward men on Jean's part.

Jean's attraction to older men seems quite clear. When she was sixteen she had her first affair with a forty-year-old man, and she enjoyed it. For the most part, all her male lovers since that time have been considerably older. The younger ones she has gone with have not lasted long as lovers. She feels they lack maturity, depth, and understanding. She feels more secure when she is going with a man who is settled down in life and knows where he is going. Generally, this means that she ends up with a married man. This she actually prefers, because married men make few demands on her, either in terms of time or commitment. It appears Jean is looking for some kind of father substitute. She prefers older men who are settled in life, whom she cannot dominate. She dislikes men who profess to love her too much and who state they will do anything for her. She could not dominate her father, and although he loved her, there was never any doubt about her not being able to dominate him.

Jean's relationship with her mother was quite different. She could confide in her and have no fear about discussing her life with her. Her mother was warm and feminine. She usually took Jean's side in arguments with her father. There was considerable physical contact between them, so from her earliest childhood, Jean felt comfortable with another woman's touch. Her mother liked sex and seemed to transmit this to her daughter.

It is not surprising that Jean prefers women, but at the same time is attracted to men. She associates warmth, tenderness, and affection with women, and domination and struggle with men. In her discussion of why she prefers women in bed, she says that women will know what she wants, which in a way is repeating the understanding she received from her mother. She wants a man who is strong and knows what he wants, and that comes from her father. If she wants both of them, she can solve it by being bisexual.

She does not like men who are jealous, or in other words, possessive. Her perception is that only bisexual men fit into this category. Not wanting to possess or own her, they are then free to discuss things as equals, even their own love affairs. This raises the question of the "normalcy" of jealousy. One argument is that jealousy is inextricably tied with love, so one must have the one with the other. It follows that if one is not jealous, one does not love the other person. This certainly leads to two people being tied to one another, and to a great restriction of one's actions. There are many men who are jealous not only of other men, but of their wives' women friends. There are men who are jealous of the time their wives spend with their own children. The other argument is that true love has no room for jealousy, that jealousy is a lack of faith and without faith their is no love. This point of view can lead to "open marriage," for each individual completely determines his own actions.

One must take one position or the other and from that determine if Jean's evaluation of the bisexual man as being without jealousy is "normal" or not. If you say jealousy has no part in a sexual relationship, then Jean may be evaluating her relationships correctly. If you feel jealousy is tied to love, then she has misinterpreted her men and is chasing an impossible scheme.

Coming back to our original operational definition of bisexuality, I would be forced to say that Jean was a functioning bisexual and gives every appearance of continuing along these lines for some time to come. In addition, she appears to be doing so without any guilt. That is apparent.

7

Sam

I meet Sam at his office in Century City in West Los Angeles. He's running late with his patients, and his nurse asks me to have a seat in the waiting room. "The doctor will be with you as soon as he can." I sit down and leaf through some magazines while three curious women try to figure out what I'm doing there.

After his last patient, Sam suggests we drive out to his house for a drink. "We can get in a swim, too. I could use one. This has been a hell of a day. I had surgery this morning and a breech delivery at noon and five extra women who just had to be slipped in! I should have been a dermatologist."

On the ride home I ask, "But you like obstetrics and gynecology?"

"Oh, yes. I even like the hectic part of it. This is just a bad time for me."

He lives in a small house in Coldwater Canyon. There's one bedroom, a study, a living-dining doom, and a small kitchen. The house forms a U around a patio and pool, and he lends me trunks for a late dip. Sam does laps for fifteen minutes, and then collapses into a beach chair near mine. "I needed that!" He pats his flat stomach. "I'm out of condition."

Actually, for a forty-year-old man he looks very fit. His short blond hair is bleached by the California sun, and his lean body is tanned and well-muscled. His features are Dutch, from his blue eyes to his cleft chin, and I can see how popular he must be as a woman's doctor.

"On the ride here you said this was a bad time."

"Let me get you a drink." He walks to a bar and refrigerator on the patio and mixes us two gin and tonics. Sitting down with a sigh, he stirs his drink and says, "If you had been here a month ago I would have told you I was one happy guy. I really thought I had it made."

"Why?"

"Well, I was in love with two wonderful people, and they both loved me. My work was going well—hell, I thought I was having my cake and eating it."

"What happened?"

He turns his glass in his hands. "I got my walking papers from both in the same week."

"Do they both live in Los Angeles?"

"No. Linda lives up the coast on the Monterey Peninsula near Carmel. It's funny, I met her in Washington, D.C., about two years ago. I was there on a medical convention, and I attended a party for the Peace Corps. She was working for them, recruiting. We got along very well, and I made her promise to get in touch with me if she ever came out West. She did, about a month later. She came on business, and then took a week's vacation, and I was able to take off, too. We had a fantastic time. We found we loved all the same things, swimming, golfing—she fell in love with the

Big Sur country and swore she'd come out here someday
to live."

"What does she look like?"

He smiles. "Nothing like me. She's a tiny thing, small-
boned, with black hair and eyes. She's half-Spanish and
half-American-Indian, and she was raised in the South, in
Virginia. She's really remarkable, the kind of woman men
stop to stare at in the street or in restaurants—she gets attention wherever she goes."

"Do you mind that?"

He shakes his head emphatically. "I love it! It's as if
everyone who looks at her envies me."

"What sort of person is she?"

"She's very shy, though she gives an impression of self-
assurance. She hasn't dated many men, and although I
didn't know it at the time, most of her male friends were
gay."

"She could accept that?"

"I think she felt safer with them. She had dated one man
for years, and then they broke up and he married someone
else. She was very shaken by it—I guess she felt betrayed.
Anyway, when I met her she was reluctant to get into any
kind of deep relationship. She didn't want to get involved
sexually or emotionally."

"But she did with you?"

"Not right away." He shivers and gets up to take some
towels from a closet at the end of the patio. "Here. It's
getting chilly." He drapes one over his shoulders and mixes
another drink. "I didn't see her for almost a year after that,
although we wrote. That was when I became involved with
Charlie."

"Tell me about him."

He scratches his head. "Charlie had just separated from
his wife. They were married—let's see—thirteen years. I
guess that's an unlucky number. Charlie works for a drug
company as a detail man, a salesman, and he came to my

office to fill me in on some drugs. We liked each other and it was the end of the day, so we just kept talking." He laughs, remembering. "My nurse took off and we were still yakking. We didn't have any idea of the time, and it was almost ten before we realized it. It was crazy. I guess we were both lonely, and we hit it off. We had dinner together and one thing led to another." He pauses, and after a long silence I ask, "What was Charlie like?"

He looks at me, his eyes clouded, his face very vulnerable. He suddenly seems much younger than forty. "A lot like Linda physically. Slight and dark—he was Jewish, born in Germany. He came here with his parents, refugees from the Nazis when he was just a kid. Let's see—I think his father died during World War Two, but his mother's still around. Charlie was a pre-med who didn't make it. He went into drug detailing. It's a shame. He'd have made a good doctor, a hell of a lot better one than me."

"Why?"

Sam shrugs. "He had a lot of empathy. He could really understand people. You felt it just being with him. He's great with his children. He has two boys, one is eight and the other is ten, and he's very close to them." He smiles. "We used to go out to the beach with them on Sundays— he had custody over the weekends."

"What happened to his marriage?"

Sam shrugs. "The way he tells it, it fell apart. I gather she knew he liked sex with men before they were married, and he told me he only had a few affairs afterward, during his marriage, but he said things got to the point where she was tormenting him sexually and emotionally. He claimed she had the kids only to hold him."

"But he left his wife before you met him."

He looks up suddenly, startled. "Well, yes, sure. He didn't leave her over me." Ruefully, he say, "I don't think I meant that much to him."

"Have you always been bisexual?"

He shakes his head slowly. "No. At one time I was only heterosexual. I just went with women. I'm not even sure I knew that much about homosexuality, except as a sort of distant thing to make fun of. There were no homosexuals in our home town that I knew of."

"Where was that?"

"A little Pennsylvania Dutch town in Amish country. My folks came from Amish stock originally."

"What were they like?"

"Very nice—what are parents like?" He laughs. Let's see. I had two brothers, one nine years younger and one nine years older. What does that tell you about my parents?"

"They were very cautious."

He lifts his eyebrows. "You hit it on the head. Cautious, careful, middle-class, never get into a position of financial instability, never do anything that would make talk in the community, never spend money extravagantly. With the three of us spaced out like that, our education didn't break my father. My younger brother is a lawyer and my older brother's a doctor, too, a surgeon. I think as a kid I was closer to my mother, but when I got older I really discovered my father. He was a very quiet, very thoughtful man, an insurance salesman. I could never talk to him, I mean really talk, but what kid can talk to his father? No, there was never any trouble between us, but—" He pauses, frowning a little. "There was never any real closeness, not like there is between Charlie and his kids. I've seen him pick them up and hug them, throw them around and laugh with them. My father never did that to us." His voice has become wistful, almost sad. "But he was a good man," he adds quickly, defensively.

"Your parents are still alive?"

"Oh, yes. They'll go on into their nineties. We're a long-lived family."

"Are you close to your brothers?"

He shakes his head. "Not very. There are too many years

between us. One was always too old and the other too young. I like them, and their families, they're both married, but they live back East and I rarely see them."

"Did you date many girls in school?"

"Not many in high school. I don't think I had much of a sexual drive, but in college I went hog-wild. Maybe because I was away from home. I went to Berkeley, you know, and by the end of my freshman year I had sex—I kept count—with twenty girls. That's pretty good for a college freshman." He says it without boasting, sort of sadly.

"Did you enjoy it?"

"Yes—" He hesitates. "A lot of it was the quick fraternity sex where you really don't know what the hell you're doing, but there were two or three deeper affairs, girls I thought I was in love with—and maybe I was. I think it put an end to the indiscriminate sex. I guess it was finding out what sex could really be like."

"When did you first sleep with a man?"

He stands up abruptly. "Let's get some clothes on. It's getting chilly."

We dress, and after Sam makes fresh drinks we sit down in the living room. Leaning back in a club chair, he says, "You asked me about the first man I had sex with. It was kind of an upsetting experience."

"How did it happen?"

"Well, I had graduated from med school and I had a summer off before I started internship—that was back in 1958. My father gave me a graduation gift, a round-trip ticket to Europe, and I bummed my way down to the Mediterranean and crossed to Israel. I really loved Israel, and I even thought I might practice there someday. I tell you, if I were Jewish I might have gone back, but I don't think a Christian M.D. would stand much chance. Anyway, I was in Jerusalem, and a friend took me to the Turkish baths there —the real Turkish baths. They're fabulous.

"There was one guy there who kept looking at me, and it made me uneasy. I told my friend, and he said, 'You're crazy. It's just that you're the only blond here.' Well, he was wrong, because this guy followed me around and made a pass at me in the steam room."

"What did you do?"

"I was very nervous and I guess close to panic. I told my friend I had to leave, and I'd meet him at his place later. I got out in a hurry, but so did the fellow who made the pass at me. He said he wanted to apologize, and would I have coffee with him?"

"What was he like?"

"Very tall and dark, with a big mustache—a very handsome guy—and he spoke English well. We had coffee and talked."

"How did you feel?"

"Mixed up. On the one hand, I was really scared about the whole thing, and at the same time, I was curious, very curious and attracted to him. I was afraid of that attraction, too. He finally talked me into going home with him, and we ended up in bed. I had just never done anything like that before. I didn't understand what was going on inside myself."

"Did it upset you?"

"You're damned right. I was like some girl who's lost her virginity. I cried for almost an hour. But he was a very decent guy and he kind of talked me out of it, or over it." Sam is quiet for a while, then says, "He wanted me to see him again, but I left that night. I hadn't planned to, but I felt I just had to get away. I was all torn up and confused, and sure that everyone who looked at me could tell I was queer. I went through all kinds of hell."

"What happened then?"

He finishes his drink and puts it down. "I came back to the States as soon as I could get a flight, and I had a day's layover in New York. I was still shook up, but I went for a walk and let someone pick me up and I went home with him, just like that."

"Did you enjoy it?"

"I don't know. I was in a terrible state. I threw up in the guy's bedroom and felt guilty and angry at myself." He laughs harshly. "When I got back to my hotel I decided I would commit suicide, but I didn't have either the means or the guts. Instead I went out and got very drunk." He falls silent, and after a long pause, I ask, "What happened?"

He shrugs. "Someone else picked me up and took me home. I don't remember anything except waking up in his bed and somehow all my conflict seemed silly."

"How do you mean?"

"Well, I think I just decided, if I was homosexual, O.K., I was homosexual. I'd make the most of it. I went back home and then to the hospital out here where I took my internship, convinced I was gay. For two years I went out with men only."

"And yet you went into obstetrics and gynecology?"

He smiles at that. "I never said I didn't like women. I do. I always have. No, ob-gyn work was what I wanted to do, and I did it."

"What about your folks?"

"Well, I told them. You see, I thought I was exclusively homosexual, that I wouldn't ever have anything to do with women sexually, and I wanted them to know."

"How did they take it?"

He wets his lips and sighs. "Pretty well, considering their background. They were upset, but we talked it over, and eventually my father said all he really wanted was for me to be happy, and if this was the life I wanted, O.K. The only thing he made me promise was that I'd see a psychiatrist. He promised to pay for it."

"Did you?"

"For a couple of years. It helped me—not in terms of my sexuality, I don't think I had any conflict there, I just thought I had—but in terms of my life itself. I had gotten pretty wild sexually with men, the way I had been with women during my freshman year at college. I was jumping into bed indiscriminately with every guy who'd have me. That calmed down after a year of therapy."

"But you stopped after two years?"

"Yeah. After my internship and residency I settled down here in L.A. I was a lot more discreet. I guess I was concerned about my practice, my hospital connections. I had an affair with a male nurse at Harbor Hospital and we were almost caught. That sobered me up. I began to wonder just what the hell I was up to. What the hell was I trying to prove? I'd done enough medical reading to know that most homosexuals are promiscuous, and here I was, falling right into that pattern."

It had grown dark out, and he switches on a table lamp that gives a warm yellow glow to the room. Then he walks to the wall and throws a switch and a series of lights in the pool makes the water glow and lights the terrace indirectly. I admire the effect, and he stares out at the pool for a moment, then sits down.

"I love it here, I really do. One of my gay friends designed the terrace and helped me decorate the house. That was way back when I finished my residency. I was still in my homosexual stage then—at least that's how I think of it now."

"But you stopped being promiscuous, sexually?"

"Yes, but I had become more than just sexually promiscuous, I had taken on the protective coloring of the homosexual."

"What do you mean?"

He gestures vaguely. "You know, talking like one—the whole limp-wrist bit—jewelry, pinkie rings, I.D. bracelets.

I think what finally brought me up short was an older doctor in the L.A. area turning me down on a partnership deal. He was in an office setup with another man, and they were looking for a third. It was a good deal financially, and the kind of practice I wanted. But after he met me he said no. I couldn't understand it because I had all the credentials they wanted, and then some friend tipped me off. He hadn't liked my manner. What he actually said, I found out later, was, 'I don't want no goddamned fag as a partner.' "

"Did that upset you?"

"It goddamned well did, but it also set me thinking. What the hell was I doing to my life? I thought of going back into therapy, and then I thought, hell, if I can't work this out myself, maybe I deserve to get out of medicine and become an out-and-out fag!"

"What did you do?"

His voice has a satisfied edge to it. "I straightened up and cut out all the crap. I knew that I really didn't want to be gay, with all it implied. I think, in a sense, I was punishing myself, saying, if this is what you're going to do, then suffer a little by having people ridicule you. What I really wanted was to be a doctor and have my own practice, and I knew damned well I had to act straight to do it, so I straightened up." He smiles at his own pun.

"You started your own practice?"

"Actually, I bought into someone else's. My older brother loaned me the money. This was a doctor who was going to retire, and we worked together for a year—and then the poor guy had a heart attack and died, and I took over the practice. It's a good deal, a little hectic, but I like it. Eventually, I suppose I'll take in a partner."

"Did you become involved with Charlie while you were still in your homosexual phase?"

"Oh, no—no. That only lasted a year or so. When I went into partnership with Dr. Goldfarb I met an O.R. nurse at the hospital—an Irish woman about five years older than me. We liked each other, and I always used to get her to work with me." He falls silent, chewing at his lip for a while, then sighs. "One morning we had a hysterectomy that was a real bitch. It was cancer and it had spread through the entire pelvis. I should have sewn her up without touching her, but I tried to clean her out, to do a pelvic exenteration. It was hopeless. We worked for hours, and she died on the table, mercifully. I don't think I've ever been so shook."

"What happened?" I ask.

"Kitty and I went out afterward and got stoned, blind drunk, and I ended up at her apartment, in her bed. To me it was the final eye opener."

"How do you mean?"

"Well, I had myself figured for a homosexual, and here I go home with a woman, blind drunk, and have sex—and it was good. We spent the next day in bed. I canceled all my appointments, and she called in sick, and we just screwed the day away." He shakes his head wonderingly. "It's hard to explain, but we both were sort of desperate. Maybe it was that poor woman dying after we had tried like hell to keep her alive, but whatever it was, we needed each other."

"How long did your affair with her last?"

"It never was an affair. We had a need, a real, heartbreaking need at that time, at that moment, and we went to bed together to satisfy it. We never did it again, but for me— it just brought me to my senses. I realized that I was no more homosexual than I was heterosexual. That was a big turning point for me."

"In what way?"

"In every way. It ended that whole compulsive period, along with my conviction that I was gay. I realized that I could want—need—sex with a woman, and after that things were different."

"Different how?"

He shrugs. "Basically, I stopped avoiding women. I took sex when and where I found it. If I met a guy and I liked him, O.K., I'd sleep with him. If I met a girl I liked, I'd have an affair with her. It became a matter of who, not what. It was the individual first; the sex was a secondary attribute of the person. You know what I mean?"

I said, "Yes, I think I do."

Leaning back, he crosses his legs and laughs. "One thing I managed to do. I was having an extended affair with a young actress out here, really a nice kid, warm and outgoing, but both of us knew it wasn't a permanent thing. She was too involved in her career, with a capital C. Well, she was going East for some commercials in New York, and I had some free time about then, so I flew East with her and took her to see my parents."

Surprised, I ask, "Why, if it wasn't serious?"

"Well, I wanted them to realize I was out of the 'men only' stage, and I thought this was a nice way to do it."

"What happened?"

He smiles as he remembers. "It was a good thing. I explained that Ann and I weren't serious, but we were kind of living together, and my mom looked on Ann as a savior who had snatched me from the jaws of homosexuality. Even Dad was overwhelmed. Usually he's very quiet, but he couldn't do enough for Ann. It's funny. We split up long ago, though we're still friends, but she keeps in touch with my folks, letters and Christmas cards."

He leaves me for a few minutes to put on some coffee, and eventually I follow him into the kitchen, a small, pleasant room with a faintly Spanish look. I sit at the table and he brings some mugs and plugs in an electric percolator. Looking about the room, I say, "It's very neat for a bachelor."

He follows my gaze and shrugs. "No credit to me. I have a woman who comes in for a few hours each morning while

I'm at the office. She cleans and does the wash and usually leaves some supper if I'm going to eat in. Heat-and-eat stuff—she's a jewel."

"What's your social life like here?"

"Oh, very active. Most of my friends are movie people, writers, directors, a few actors. Some of the neighbors are in real estate—but there's a lot of socializing, a lot of partying, and I love it. I'm very social myself." He pours the coffee and takes some cream from the refrigerator. "I go to Aspen now and then for the skiing, and a friend up the canyon has a beautiful tennis court. I find it a great life for a single man."

"Do you see yourself settling down and getting married?"

He moves restlessly. "I don't know. How can I tell now? I love children. I was crazy about Charlie's two kids, but I'm troubled by the idea of being tied to one person for life. It's scary. It's like owning another person."

"But most people do get married."

Frowning, he says, "In my field you find out that most marriages are basically unhappy. Half of my women patients get a crush on me because their own lives are so empty, their relations with their husbands so meaningless."

"But your parents' marriage has been good."

"They're an exception." He hesitates. "On the surface their marriage seems good, but I don't know. I'd hate to live their kind of life."

"Why?"

He gestures vaguely. "It seems so sterile, so empty. There they are, isolated in rural Pennsylvania, Mom with the house and garden—she really doesn't know anything else—and Dad with his insurance. That's the extent of their life, it's limits. That's frightening to me!"

"Did you consider a steady relationship with Charlie? Living together?"

He is quiet for a moment, turning his coffee mug. "We

talked about it many times, but neither of us wanted to give up his freedom. And then, well, very few of my friends know I'm bisexual. Out here, of course, homosexuality is no big deal. It seems to me that about half the men I meet are available, but bisexuality is something else. People draw back from it. It's a little, well, sick to most. I don't think it would be too good for my practice."

"That's very important to you?"

Intently, he says, "More important than anything else! That's another thing. When I marry someone, or live with someone, they would have to subordinate their entire life to that."

"Why?"

"It would just work out that way. My life is tied to it that closely."

"So Charlie wasn't involved with your friends?"

"No, not really, nor I with his. We saw each other during the week. Usually in the evenings and at his place. Then we'd take time off together. We played golf a great deal, but his weekends were taken up with the kids and he preferred to be with them exclusively, and eventually my weekend were taken up with Linda."

"How did that happen?"

"Well, she had come out here without telling me. She had been very taken with the country when she first came, and she pulled strings to get reassigned. When a chance came up, she took it and rented a place near Carmel. When she was settled in, she called me."

"Were you surprised?"

"I was stunned. Really shook up. I was involved with Charlie and I thought I was in love with him—well, I guess I was—and then, hearing from Linda, I suddenly realized how much I had missed her, how much I wanted to see her. I told her I'd be up that night, and I drove up after hours, it was a Friday evening, and I remember I had the car radio on and there was an opera on, and I was singing along like a maniac." He chuckles as he tells it. "I was just that happy!"

"What happened when you saw her?"

"It was great. We went out to dinner and we were like two kids. She kept asking me, 'Are you sure you're not upset that I came out here like this without telling you?' and when I assured her I wasn't, she said, 'I wasn't going to call you.' And I said, 'Why not?' and she said, 'I don't want to tie you down,' and then she began crying and I had to reassure her I was glad she had come, and I was, believe me. Then we were both laughing again."

He pours another cup of coffee and frowns at the cup. "We spent most of Saturday in bed making love, and Sunday we went swimming on a lonely stretch of beach and talked for hours."

"Did you tell her about Charlie?"

"Yes. It was terribly hard for me, but to my amazement it didn't matter to her at all. That was when she told me she had always dated gay men because she felt more comfortable with them, and I told her I wasn't gay, and she said she knew that. Anyway, it was sort of the icing on the cake."

"What do you mean?"

"Well, getting together with her was wonderful enough, but the fact that I could be honest, that I didn't have to lie about Charlie—you don't know how much that meant to me."

"And Charlie?"

"What do you mean?"

"Well, did you tell him?"

He frowns. "No. I just couldn't, and anyway, I felt there was no need to. He was just as happy if we didn't get together on weekends. Then he could devote all his time to his kids, and what the hell, we saw each other during the week, two or three nights at least, and we still took time off now and then for golfing or skiing."

"But in effect you were leading a double life."

"Yes." He considers. "I guess you could call it that. Linda understood, and she had an active life of her own. She still works for the Peace Corps, and she travels a great deal, but every weekend that she was here I saw her. Her place was like a refuge for me. We'd rent horses and ride into the hills, or take long hikes along the beach—I was so goddamned happy."

"In both your affairs?"

"Oh, yes. There was something every quiet about Linda, very—" He searches for the right word. "Restful? No, that's so flat. I could drive up there after an exhausting week and unwind in three hours."

"And with Charlie?"

He laughs. "Things were never quiet. We argued a lot. I think it was usually my fault."

"Why?"

He moves his shoulder uncomfortably. "I used to push too much, testing him, I guess. I'd try and get him to give up a weekend with his kids, as if I was forcing him to choose between us when I knew he wouldn't, and I really didn't want him to. I wanted to be with Linda anyway, but still, I was jealous of him."

"Why? Was he involved with other men?"

"I don't think so, at least not now. But I used to get all sorts of crazy ideas. I'd convince myself that he was playing around, that he had other lovers. Once I even drove to his house after work and parked a block away watching the house."

"What happened?"

He grimaces. "The cops stopped by and made me identify myself and move on. I told them I felt dizzy and was parking until I felt better. It was a hell of an embarrassing situation."

"It doesn't sound as if things were so great between you."

He looks up at me quizzically. "Don't get the wrong idea. For the most part they were, and I even enjoyed the hassling in a funny way. I really think that we loved each other—at least I loved him." He hesitates. "And I'm sure he loved me, at least until he found out about Linda."

"How did that happen?"

"Most of my friends knew about her, and occasionally she'd come down on weekends for a party or a social event and stay over at the house." He spreads his hands in a sort of hopeless gesture. "I guess it was inevitable. She stayed over one Sunday and had an appointment in San Diego on Monday. She came back afterward and Charlie showed up. She was pretty decent, but it was obvious to him what was going on. Oh, hell, I guess a lot of it was my fault. I wanted Charlie to know and I wanted him to accept it. I even had these crazy fantasies that the three of us would live together."

"What happened?"

"It was a very stiff Monday night, let me tell you. I proceeded to handle things in my own inimitable way by getting smashed and passing out. Charlie and Linda had a heart-to-heart talk and put me to bed, then they both left."

"And then," I prompt when he falls silent.

His voice is painful. "Charlie couldn't forgive me, I don't know whether it was because I had deceived him or because I loved Linda. God knows. We had a big blowup, and he told me it was all over. I wouldn't accept that and—oh, hell, it dragged on for another month, big soul-searching scenes and arguments and then reconciliation and lovemaking, and always the lovemaking was a little too desperate, too frantic."

He wets his lips and sighs. "Last week we had a serious, mature, quote, talk, and Charlie told me we had to break up. He had to sort things out. For one thing, he felt we had gotten too close, too involved with each other." He laughs a bit harshly. "He said it had become too much like his marriage, and he was scared. He didn't want another scene like that, so he suggested we cool it."

He stands up and brings in a bottle of brandy from the living room. "I could use a drop. How about you?" I refuse, but take another cup of coffee, and Sam pours himself a healthy glass of brandy.

"Had you been seeing Linda that month?" I ask.

"I saw her twice, and she was genuinely sorry about Charlie, but it wasn't her fault. Still, things were kind of awkward between us, and then, a few days after Charlie gave me my walking papers, Linda called and asked me not to come up that weekend. I asked why, and she said she just wanted to sort things out, to re-evaluate our relationship, a bunch of crap like that. I kept pressing her, telling her finally I'd drive up anyway and we could talk things over, and she got very upset, burst into tears, and then told me, please not to come because there was someone else. Christ, it was like being kicked in the stomach."

He finishes his glass of brandy with a grimace and offers me the bottle. When I shake my head he pours himself another. "I've always hated rejection. Maybe that's why losing Linda like that hit me so hard."

"And Charlie?"

"Charlie, too. Christ, if neither sex works out maybe I ought to give up the whole mess and devote myself to medicine." He laughs and takes a hearty slug of the brandy. "At least that's something I'm good at. You know, when you deliver a baby, you're a hero in the mother's eyes. You're really something."

"Is that important?"

He turns his glass, considering the brandy, and in the overhead light I suddenly see that his eyes are full. "Christ, yes!" he says tensely. "What else means anything in life? If you're something in someone else's eyes—a hero to anyone—

nobody can hurt you. Nobody can touch you. You can take any loss."

We're both quiet then, and he sits there with the tears welling up in his eyes while I am too embarrassed to speak. Finally, awkwardly, I say, "I'll have a shot of that brandy now."

He passes me one and matches it, then wipes his eyes with his sleeve. "I'm sorry, but I think I've had too much to drink."

"That's all right. I'll find my way out." Near the door I see two pictures in standing frames on a low table. One is a very lovely, thin-faced woman, and the other an intense, serious-faced man with dark heavy brows. I pick them up and Sam comes up behind me. "That's Linda and Charlie. I guess I'll put them away now. There should be a drawer somewhere in the house for old lovers."

I drive off to my hotel, feeling sad.

Sam's bisexual life and the way he describes it bring us to a larger question, an old one discussed by both professionals and laymen: what is "normal" behavior? There is a serious problem here. Is normal what the majority of people believe or do, or is it some objective standard that exists independently of what people do? It is not an easy question to answer. In a mental hospital where the majority of patients believe they are being persecuted, would persecution be "normal"? During the times of Hitler, when the majority of Germans exhibited sadistic behavior toward Jews, would that behavior be called "normal"? I do not think so.

What was considered normal sexual behavior a few decades ago has changed radically. Twenty years ago oral sex was thought of as immoral. At that time, almost all types of intercourse other than the standard missionary position were avoided by the majority as being abnormal. Today this is rapidly changing. Most sexologists have adopted a relative theory in reference to sexual activities. They believe any-thing between two consenting people is normal. Many have extended this acceptance to include homosexual activities. The American Psychiatric Association has removed homo-sexual activity from its "sick" list.

For some strange reason this has not been extended to bi-sexual relations. In our interviews we encountered a strange reluctance to admit to bisexual relations. One would think that with our changing morality this would not be the case. But there is a great fear of being discovered on the part of bisexuals. It is the same type of fear we found in homo-sexuals over ten years ago. Bisexuals feel a revelation will bring with it instant rejection.

I believe we have to look into the culture to discover the reasons for this. No matter how strongly the concept of cultural relativity has taken hold in our culture, it certainly has not reached the world of the bisexual. Deeply embedded in our country is an old-fashioned black-and-white morality —things are either right or wrong. There is an attempt to fit all things into an either/or mold, and if they do not fit, there is a tendency to reject them. Bisexuality does not fit neatly into a right or a wrong category. This causes a certain anxiety in people that leads to a rejection of bisexuality. It is as if we are saying, "I can handle it if I can put it in a pigeonhole, but if I can't, it makes me uneasy and perhaps I should do away with it."

I think the proper way to approach the morality or immo-rality of bisexuality is by looking at it as being on a sliding scale. On one end of the scale would be totally unaccept-able sexual acts, and on the other end, totally acceptable activity. At the present time, I believe bisexual activity is entering the acceptable end of the scale. As it becomes less and less anxiety-producing, it will slide closer to the totally acceptable end of the scale.

Another aspect we must take into consideration in thinking of bisexuality in any specific couple is motivation. Every human action must be viewed from the point of view of motivation. If the motivation is not correct, it is likely the end act will not be correct.

In interviews with bisexuals, I have come to the conclusion that there can be many motivations for their bisexual lives. One person may be bisexual because he is trying to cover up his basic homosexual drive with a façade of heterosexuality. Generally, he will fail because his motivation is incorrect. Or a couple may enter into bisexuality to save their failing marriage. They do not really like bisexuality, but they are reaching out for anything that might bring them together and keep them there.

Another causal factor is fear of getting too close to a member of the opposite sex. If this is present, the person can flee into bisexuality as an escape. The fear of getting too close to a member of the opposite sex may appear to be a simple thing to understand, but it isn't. What has happened is that in the life of a particular individual a series of events has occurred that has produced a fear of the opposite sex. This fear makes the person shy away from the opposite sex, because no one wants to repeat unpleasant events. Unfortunately, these fears exist in the unconscious, so they are difficult to see or to even get hold of in any particular person. They are generally not seen by the individual having them, so they are usually vigorously denied.

If this basic fear of the opposite sex is present, a person may flee into homosexual activity. I believe this may also be the reason for a certain amount of bisexual activity. The bisexual often doesn't get very close to the opposite sex. In other words, if the bisexual is fleeing from close contact with the opposite sex, he will not find much satisfaction in his sexual life because his unconscious motivation will not be satisfied.

We must, however, leave room for the minority of those

people whose drive for bisexual activity is not motivated by conflicting unconscious motivation. I believe there are some people whose drive for bisexuality must be accepted as "normal" for them. In order to do this, we have to eliminate all the possible unconscious reasons that might be pushing them beyond their conscious control into bisexuality.

To get insights into the bisexuality of Sam, we should look at what Sam thinks about himself. We can start with certain words he used about himself during our interview, and generalize from those words to his sexual life.

When he was talking about Charlie, his lover, Sam made the statement, "He'd have made a good doctor, a hell of a lot better one than me." This was the first indication that he does not think too much of himself as a doctor and even, perhaps, as a person. But at that point in the interview it would have been unwarranted to come to any conclusions.

As Sam talked further of Charlie, he said, "I don't think I meant that much to him." He was speaking here of whether Charlie had left his wife to go with Sam. Translated psychologically, this could mean that Sam doesn't see himself as being that important to any other person—at least not important enough to reject another for.

To carry our search further, Sam at one point said, "Maybe I deserve to get out of medicine and become an out-and-out fag." Here we should focus on the word "deserve" because this carries with it a judgment aspect. If one does not deserve something, he judges himself to be unworthy.

In discussing bisexuality, he said, "Very few of my friends know I'm bisexual. . . . It's sick to most." We have to at least entertain the possibility that Sam still believes himself to be sick because of his bisexual activities.

Later on, speaking of Charlie again, Sam says, "At least I loved him." This is a possible indication that he did not feel loved by Charlie in spite of their close relationship.

His motivations seem to flow to a great extent in the direction of what other people will think of him: "What else means anything in life? If you're something in someone else's eyes —a hero to anyone—nobody can hurt you. Nobody can touch you. You can take any loss." He seems to feel that being an M.D. is being a hero, so we might say his entire motivation for going into medicine may have had something to do with his feelings of wanting to be accepted by people and to protect himself from being touched by anyone.

We could take that another step forward and say it lies within the realm of possibility that his bisexual involvements are very superficial unless they satisfy this need to be thought of as a hero. When Charlie threw him aside because of Sam's excessive demands for attention, and when his girl friend discarded him for another man, he felt he was not good at anything, and playfully said perhaps he should devote himself to medicine, because, "at least that's something I'm good at."

Sam does not seem to be very good at facing a great many of the realities in his life. There is a tendency to get drunk and not meet them head-on. I would say that in spite of being in psychiatric treatment for several years, Sam has not solved his unconscious homosexual conflict and is using bisexuality as a means of avoiding it.

8

Ann and Rick

I have decided to interview Ann and Rick at my office because they both share apartments with roommates and neither would be comfortable talking to me at home. While I am waiting for them, Rick calls up from downstairs and tells me that Ann is late, but he's sure she'll show. He doesn't want to come up without her. When they finally arrive, they are almost an hour late.

The only word that describes Ann is tiny. She's about five feet tall and her features are regular and delicate. She has a beauty that grows on you as she talks, perhaps because her face in animation is so different from her face at rest. Her smile is like an inner light.

Ann wears jeans and sandals and a gauze shirt that gaps at the buttons. Through it I can see her breasts, feminine but small. Her hair is dark brown and kinky, pulled back from a center part and caught with a rubber band.

Rick is tall, and seems even taller next to Ann. In jeans

and an unpressed workshirt, he gives the impression of being well-built but not heavy. His black hair is shoulder-length and caught in a ponytail. He's a handsome young man, but a long drooping mustache hides the expression around his mouth and gives him an impassive quality. He moves slowly, and talks so quietly that his words are barely audible.

We sit in three large, black leather armchairs near the window, and I wonder how to draw them out. They have no need to talk and seem perfectly content to sit in silence. Their attitude seems to be, "If you want to know something, ask me. I'm not going to volunteer anything."

"You're not married?" I ask, and get a small negative smile. "Is it as close as that? Are you going together, or are you just good friends?"

Rick shifts in his chair. "It's kind of getting there."

"You don't live together?" Again a negative shrug. They both watch me quietly. Apprehensively? No, not even uncertainly. Just quiet, waiting. I have a sudden realization that they are both very much at ease.

"Have you always been bisexual?" I ask Rick, deciding to plunge in suddenly.

"Ah—no. I never was, before. That's when I started, when I met Ann, you know? I started off making it with her, and she was into this thing with other chicks. Like, at first, I couldn't understand it, and then I kept wondering. I kept wondering what it would be like to make it with a guy, and I guess that's when it first started for me."

"You mean that's when you first tried it?"

He shifts again in his chair and laughs a bit uncomfortably. "Yeah, but I prefer chicks. Just out of curiosity I began to get into it." He looks at Ann quickly, then, stroking his mustache, says, "I feel kind of strange, us talking about it."

I move away from men for a moment. "Was Ann the first girl you had sex with?"

"Hell, I'm twenty-three. No, there were others."

Ann laughs and Rick grins sheepishly. I come back to men. "How did it happen with your first guy?"

"Well, actually it happened with someone I knew. He's a guy who's been homosexual all his life. When me and Ann got together, when we got into this whole thing, I talked to my friend and—well, we wound up doing all sorts of things."

"Did he turn you on as much as girls did?" I ask.

Rick considers, stroking his mustache. "At first it was only curiosity, but then it was pleasure, too. I don't really know how to put it." He frowns a moment. "I have to try and find out."

"Did you like this friend of yours as a person?"

"Yeah. He was a good friend of mine for a long time."

"Did anything warmer come out of the sexual encounter?"

Rick looks over at Ann thoughtfully. "No. I don't really think so. We were close friends, but that was all. He did his thing, and I did mine." He hesitates. "But afterward we really became closer friends. We do a lot of things together now."

"Then you feel it's been a good experience?"

Again Rick considers. "Yeah."

"Have you had any other experiences with men?"

"Yeah."

"How many?"

"Twice." His answers are sufficient, but he contributes almost nothing without my pulling it out of him, and yet I feel there is no real reluctance to talk. This is Rick, and in some way I haven't yet hit the right question.

"Have these experiences with other men been good?" I ask.

Again he considers a moment before he answers. "Actually I haven't made it more than once with one of them. The other guy, we've made it with each other a few times, and that's been it. I keep looking, when I want it. I go to these gay clubs down in the Village, to this place called Danny's and the Village Vanguard. Gay people hang out there."

"Are you attracted to any particular type of man?"

Again he considers. "No—not really."

I try to make my question clearer. "Do you like a man who's masculine or one who's feminine?" He seems unable to answer, and I offer a suggestion. "Or is it just the person that you get to like?"

He picks up on that quickly. "Yeah, it's just the person that I get to like. I like a person. Then I'd like to make it with him. I don't like someone, and no matter what he's like I couldn't make it."

Ann is smiling, and I ask, "How about you, Ann?"

"Me?"

"Well, how did you get into bisexuality?"

There is no hesitation about Ann's answers. She speaks quickly and positively in a beautifully modulated voice. There is none of Rick's hesitancy. "I started out bi, and I really don't know which I preferred, so I started making it with two people at the same time, a chick and a guy. Actually, they were my friends, and they were married. She was about twenty-five and he was maybe thirty. It worked out. It was good, but I realized that I enjoyed it with guys more. I mean I enjoyed it with him more than with her."

Puzzled, I ask, "But then, why bisexuality?"

"Well, you know, I wanted to give it another chance. So I made it with chicks again, with a couple of close girl friends who are bisexual. I still do, but I also make it with Rick all the time, whenever we're together. Still, when I want to have a change . . ." Her voice trails off and she smiles at Rick, who pivots in his chair and smiles back.

"Do you make it with girls alone as well as couples?"

"Sure."

"Which do you prefer?"

"Well, I've done it with a lot of people. In fact, I like having orgies, but only when we're all participating. You know, I find that if I have a close girl friend and I make it with her, it makes us even closer. We can be better friends because, well, there's no barrier at all. If you can touch someone, you can communicate with them."

"Are you saying it makes a more honest relationship?"

"Oh, definitely, because they're not hiding their physical desires."

"Have you and Rick been in a relationship with another guy or girl?"

Ann laughs, and Rick smiles sheepishly. Mischievously, she says, "I tried, but he couldn't make it. I brought him with me to a couple's house one time, but he didn't participate. He just sat there and watched."

"Why didn't you participate?" I ask Rick.

He shrugs. "First off, I was kind of nervous. I wasn't sure. I didn't know, did I want to do this, and was it wrong? Now—well, now I really don't think it's wrong."

Ann interrupts. "When you do one thing all your life, and you're told that's the only way to do it, anything else seems wrong. We're all told the right way is with the other sex. The right way is to get married, to have children."

"I went to Catholic school half my life," Rick explains.

"Are you both Catholic?" I ask.

"I'm an atheist," Rick says flatly.

"I mean were you born a Catholic?"

"Yeah."

"And you?" I ask Ann.

"I was born a Christian Scientist. They're very big on marriage, but not sex. Maybe that's why I wanted to try something different, just because I was told not to. Hell, what you're told you can't have, you want."

I agree with that. "It has to be good if you can't have it."

"Sure, because otherwise, why can't you have it?"

"Tell me what it was like when you were a kid," I ask Ann. "What were your parents like?"

"My mother was a Christian Scientist, but my father was an atheist. Still, he never objected to my mother's religion. He kind of went along with it. Let's see. My sister is younger than me, and my brother is older. We grew up in a small town in the Midwest, and I guess it was a regular good clean American household. You did something wrong, you got spanked. You went to Christian Science school, you read your lessons, you went to church, high school, college— everything that was expected of you."

"When did you first have any kind of sex?"

"When I was in the seventh grade. I was curious and a guy in my class was curious, too. We both wanted to know what it was like, so we went off to a place in the woods he knew and—well, we didn't really know what we were doing. We tried things out and experimented, and to me it wasn't all that great. We were just kids."

"Were you sexually active in college?"

She shakes her head. "I never went to college. I just finished high school and picked up and left my family."

"Why did you leave?"

Ann shrugs. "They just couldn't agree with my way of living. They laid down very rigid laws. I have to live at home, not date, be in at a certain hour, go to college, and fit into a mold they made. I didn't want to, so I left, as simple as that."

It didn't seem simple to me. "A lot of people are forced into a mold and feel exactly the way you did, but very few pick up and leave, especially at high-school age. How did you come to do it?"

"Maybe it was easier because I had some friends in the ninth grade who had moved to New York. When I left I came to them, and they found me a job while I stayed at their apartment."

"Are you still with them?"

"I'm on my own now."

"How did you come to meet Rick?"

Ann tucks her legs up under her, looking like a lost waif in the big leather armchair. "We met at a party and my friends were his friends and I kept seeing him around—you know, just as a friend—and I kept wondering if he was involved with my other friends, I mean, making it with them, because when I like a guy I usually want him to make it with us, I mean if I like a couple and I like a guy, making it brings us all closer together. You see, if you both understand it, then it's not out of the ordinary or abnormal."

"Is bisexuality common among your friends?"

"Some are straight, some are gay, and I guess most of them are bi."

"Your first sexual experience was with the couple you lived with, right?"

"Right."

"How old were you then?"

"I was sixteen."

"Did you enjoy it?"

"I enjoyed it very much or I wouldn't have continued it."

Looking at her, so fragile and pretty, I realize that indeed she wouldn't do anything she didn't want to do. This is a very strong young woman. "But there are people who have sex without enjoying it," I say.

"If I didn't enjoy it, I wouldn't do it, and the reason I was doing it with both men and women was because I wanted to."

"Which did you enjoy most?"

"The guy, but the point is I like being with a chick, too. It's different. You know, I don't feel that you should be restricted. That's ridiculous."

"But most of us do restrict ourselves to one sex."

She leans forward intently. "Sure, and that's the old rationale. You see, the whole point of society's reasoning is that you go with guys because only guys can give you children. If you married a chick, you couldn't have children. See what I mean?"

I consider that. "Yes, but aren't you putting the cart before the horse? If you go with a person and love that person, then you want children with that person."

Frowning, Ann says, "Yes, but you see, why are you supposed to go out with the opposite sex? Because eventually there will be marriage and children. That's how life continues. But me, I've got a lot of attitudes." She pauses for a long moment, then says, "I know what I feel when I make it with a chick. I can give her satisfaction because I know what I like sexually, and I know she's going to like the same thing."

"But if you really love a man," I argue, "and he really loves you, won't you both get to the point where you'll know what the other likes sexually and do it?"

"Oh, definitely." She hesitates, then adds disarmingly, "But I like seeing the chick's reactions, too."

"Then it's not just the technical female sexual know-how, knowing how to turn a woman on, but also the fact that you're attracted to another woman."

"Yes." Ann considers, and then, rather honestly, adds, "And maybe it's even more important that I'm not supposed to do it."

"Do you think the forbidden angle is a strong factor?"

She shakes her head. "I don't know. I really don't think so, because I enjoy doing it both ways." She reaches out and takes Rick's hand. "Take our relationship. We're very close, and it's not just sexual. When I make it with a chick, it's either a good friend, and afterward we're even better friends, or it's just someone I make it with, and that's that. But I like making it with Rick. I don't usually make it with other guys unless they're good. Mostly it's just Rick."

"But there are other men."

"Sometimes," she says reluctantly.

"Do you feel any jealousy?" I ask Rick.

Stroking his mustache, he considers. "At first I guess I felt jealous, but when I got into it myself, the jealousy just seemed to slip away."

Seriously, Ann says, "I think you didn't understand at first."

He nods emphatically. "Especially growing up and going to Catholic school. They really punch this shit into your head, all this sex and sin stuff."

"What was it like growing up?" I ask. "I mean what was your childhood like?"

Rick reaches back and unties his ponytail, letting his hair down to his shoulders. He shakes his head to make his hair fall into place. "I was born here in Manhattan on Columbus Avenue, and, like, you know, it wasn't so easy. A lot of hassles on the street. My mother split and my father took care of us—the best he could."

"How many were there?"

"Five. Me, my brother, and three girls."

"Who was the oldest?"

"My brother. I have a younger sister and two older ones." He laughs and shakes his head. "My oldest sister made it with a chick for the first time two weeks ago."

"Had she been with a man before?" I ask.

Surprised, he says, "Oh sure. She's got a three-year-old daughter."

"How did she get involved with another woman?" I ask.

"Well, as near as I know, it all started off with two guys and two chicks in the bed, and they wound up with my sister and this other chick making it together."

"How did she feel about it?"

"She won't talk about it to me. She just says it's strange. She says I wouldn't understand, but Jenny would."

"Jenny?"

"Oh, hell, I mean Ann!" Confused, Rick spreads his hands. "Jenny was a girl I used to go with."

Ann laughs. "Now that's when I get jealous. Not when he makes it with another chick, but when he confuses my name."

Rick reddens, and I ask, "Are you really more jealous of the confusion?"

She laughs again. "I'm teasing him, but seriously, I'm not

at all jealous when Rick makes it with a guy, because I know he won't establish any kind of permanent relationship with another guy. Maybe because I wouldn't ever consider spending the rest of my life with another chick. I like making it with them, but I wouldn't consider having the same relationship I have with Rick."

"Anyway," Rick says suddenly, "I went with Jenny while I was still in high school."

"Did you finish high school?" I ask.

"No. I dropped out in the ninth grade."

"Why?"

Rick shrugs. "I got sick of it, sick of school. Anyway, I started working, and I couldn't work and go to school at the same time. I was a delivery boy for the Grand Union Supermarket. I don't think I had any friends who stayed in school." He pauses, chewing his lip and considering. "Some stayed in school, but, you know, we never saw them again. They were all doing something good."

"What did you do after Grand Union?"

"Oh, I worked at all kinds of jobs. I did porter's work for a while, and then I got a break. This friend of mine whose father sold buildings, big apartment houses, got me a job working for his father, elevator boy and doorman."

"What are you doing now?"

"Now I work for a printing company."

"And you have your own apartment?"

"I share a place with another guy, but we go our own ways. We talk to each other when it comes to rent time. It's not bad."

"Do your friends know that you're bisexual now?"

He considers that for a moment. "Some do. Most of them don't believe it. You know, I always had a lot of friends, chicks who liked chicks, guys who were gay, but I never really thought about it until I met Ann."

"But you don't seem uptight about the whole idea?"

"I'm not, except—well, I'd be up tight if certain people

knew about it, like my father and some of the guys I grew up with. Especially the ones who are married and have kids." He shakes his head wonderingly. "Wow! They'd really freak out. But I don't see most of them now because we live in different neighborhoods."

"How do you feel about the whole thing, I mean, deep inside yourself?"

Rick brushes his hair back and strokes his mustache. "At first I felt strange, but now—well, I don't think that much about it. You know, I'll have sex with another guy—I really don't think anything of it. What I'm beginning to understand is how much men can enjoy sex with other men. Like with some you might not enjoy it, and with others you might."

"Do you get something different out of each relationship?"

Frowning, Rick fumbles for an explanation. "No, it's more like you get one thing out of a man and another out of a woman, only it's not too much different. What it comes to, it depends on how you feel about the person." He sits up straight and leans forward intently. "Like I'd never have a relationship with a guy like I have with Ann. With her it's just different. Everything works out fine all the time, no matter what we do, whether it's sex or walking along holding hands or talking with each other." He pauses and leans back, but I realize he hasn't finished the thought. There's a long silence while Ann and I watch him as he sorts it out in his mind, and finally he says, so softly we can hardly hear him, "I guess the whole thing is a sexual search to find out more and more."

"About each other?"

"That's right, but also it's curiosity. I was curious. I wanted to know, but I was scared. Eventually I just tried it."

"Do your sexual relationships with other men make you feel any less masculine?" I ask curiously.

"I'm not bothered about that. Maybe I'd be bothered if the people I worked with or my relatives knew about it."

"That's not quite what I meant. On a physical plane, is it easy for you to have intercourse with another man?"

"Yeah."

"And is it easy to love another man?"

"Yeah."

I find it hard to go into the graphic details, and yet I am trying to clarify my question. "When it comes to sex with another man, do you participate completely, or are you passive? Have you learned to love another man in a physical sense?"

I am having trouble expressing myself, but Rick has no trouble understanding me. "It's the only way I can make love."

"Then you're involved. It's not a case of leaning back and having it done to you?"

"That's no fun at all."

I shrug. "And yet many men, even homosexual men, can only have sex that way." I hesitate, thinking this through. "And many heterosexual women, too."

"But in that case why do it?"

Why indeed? I try asking the question differently. "Are you able to switch roles in a relationship with another man?"

"I can take either role. I can be active or passive."

Ann interrupts to clear the point. "Of course, you have to participate. You have to get into your scene. I'd feel funny if I didn't, left out."

While I'm absorbing that, Ann says, "The thing we both find strange is how many people are bisexual. Once they know we are, all of a sudden they open up."

I nod. "Of course, it's something most people keep hidden. Society has some strict taboos about this, but how do you feel about the social dos and don'ts?"

For the first time, Rick speaks up quickly. "I pay no attention to them. Sure, there are certain things I could get in trouble if I did, and I'm careful, but things like sex I keep in my own house, and who's going to come in and tell me I can or can't?"

Ann agrees. "That's our own business. It's not up to parents or friends or religion to tell me what I can do or can't do about sex. If I enjoy it, I'm going to do it."

Rick nods in agreement, and I ask, "How come, when everyone else is locked into heterosexual roles you two have shaken them off and do what you want in terms of sex? How did you arrive at this? Surely not from your background."

With a faint smile at my obtuseness, Ann says, "But I enjoy sex, very, very much. I enjoy every aspect of it and every way to do it. There's no right or wrong way. It's healthy and good."

Sitting there, so small and delicate in the big leather armchair, her statement seems preposterous. Physically, Ann is not at all the type of woman you associate with sensuality. There is nothing of the full-blown movie star, or the Playboy bunny about her. She is almost immature, a dainty child-woman. Curious, I ask, "How did you come to feel this way?"

She purses her lips and lifts her shoulders. "How does anyone come to it? I read things. I heard things. I was always curious, and if you're curious enough about a thing, you eventually try it."

"But most people who are curious feel the taboos against bisexuality are too strong," I persist. "They feel there's a loss of masculinity or feminity in trying it, and you don't."

"Perhaps because they're insecure about themselves. I'm not."

"Why not?"

"I don't see anything wrong with it."

I turn to Rick. "But until you met Ann you only had sex with girls. Were you curious then about sex with men?"

Rick is quiet again, combing his fingers through his hair while he thinks. "Well, yeah. I was curious, but I never was close to anyone who talked about it. Before I ever did it, I thought, sure, I'd be like a faggot myself if I made it with another man, like you said before, less of a man."

"But that didn't bother you after you did it?"

"No. Maybe I worried a little at first, but then I met so many people who felt the same way—it just relieved a lot of the tension."

"You met that many bisexuals?"

"Well, mostly chicks. I know a lot of chicks who are bisexual, and guys, too. Of course a lot are just straight faggots, but a lot are bisexual."

"Does it mater to you what you're like?"

"No. If a guy wants to be gay or straight, that's his thing. I'd have an affair with any guy I liked. It's the guy I'd have to like, not what he is." Rick spreads his hands. He leans forward intently, stressing the point with hands and voice. "You see, your definition of a man is *your* definition, not society's."

Ann is nodding agreement, and when Rick pauses, I ask, "How do you feel about it? Society says what you're doing isn't womanly."

Contemptuously, Ann says, "I couldn't care less what society says. I'm not asking society to accept me. I can find enough people who are like me. Look, everyone wants to be with people who do the same thing they do. For that matter, I prefer making it with someone who's bisexual instead of gay. I don't ask, 'Are you a lesbian?' because I can usually tell, but I prefer just making it with someone who swings both ways, because then she thinks the same way I do."

I ask Rick, "Do you prefer a bisexual man to someone who's gay?"

He shakes his head. "It really doesn't matter much."

"But you prefer a bisexual woman?" I ask Ann.

"That's right. It's because we share a common background, we can understand each other better. A lesbian,

well, she begins to think it's strange that you're going with
a guy. Usually she gets jealous."

"But you don't feel jealous if Rick's involved with a man?"

"No. I told you that."

"And if he was involved with another woman?"

"I'd be jealous of another woman," Ann says definitely.
"If he went with another woman, I'd rather not know about
it. I guess that's a hang-up I can't get rid of."

"Do you think it's a case of possession?"

"Oh, definitely!"

"And with another man?"

She shakes her head. "With Rick, I know another man
couldn't take my place."

"But what if he meets a man and likes him enough to form
a lasting relationship? What if they hit it off so well they
become lovers?"

"That would be all right."

I'm puzzled. "Why?" I ask. "Logically, isn't it the same
as with a woman?"

"Maybe it's because he can never marry him," Ann says
slowly.

Rick says, "In my experience, ninety-nine out of a hundred gay relationships never work out."

"But suppose you met another guy who wasn't gay,
another bisexual, and the two of you really hit it off? What
would keep you from forming a lasting relationship with
him?"

Rick spreads his hands and very simply says, "Ann."

"But she would also keep you from forming a lasting relationship with another woman."

"Yeah."

Turning to Ann, I ask, "Is your jealousy about another
woman justified then?"

"Maybe not, but I still feel it."

Rick says, "And I'd feel the same way about her and
another man, especially if it was a relationship that kept her

away from me, or if she felt more for him than she did for me."

"Look. Look at it this way," Ann says, leaning forward. "Rick and I have a real relationship. When I go out with other chicks, it's just to bring us closer as friends, but I don't go with them as a lover. It's a change, a little sexual experience that I enjoy, not a steady thing. I don't have to go with other guys because I have Rick. In an orgy it's different. Then if he's with another chick it's O.K. But if he started going out with another chick I'd feel different."

I try to sort this out. "Are you telling me you two have a relationship beyond sex? That the sex is there and it's good, but it's also good with other people. What you two have exists only with you two?"

They both nod, and Ann says, "Exactly!"

"Do you often have sex where three of you are involved?" I ask. "You and another girl and Rick?"

Ann shakes her head. "I don't like that."

"How about another guy with you and Ann?" I ask Rick.

He considers Ann speculatively, "It hasn't happened so far, and, like, it would have to happen first before I'd know how I'd react."

"I wouldn't like it," Ann says definitely. "I wouldn't like to do it."

"Do you feel that bisexuality has affected the rest of your life?"

Ann looks at Rick and frowns. "In what way?"

"Has it had any effect on the way you live, the things you do?"

"There's more honesty," Ann says slowly. "We do what we want to do."

Rick nods his head. "Yeah. There's a whole area of deceit that's cut out." He smooths his mustache, and adds, "But it depends. It depends on who I'm with. Like, there are some people who just would never understand, so I can't be honest with them."

"Are you under any more or less pressure at work?"

He shakes his head. "It's about the same."

"When you meet someone new, do you feel freer, or able to give more of yourself?"

Rick spreads his hands. I've always felt free. I've always, you know, done what I wanted to. I just wanted sex with another man. After knowing Ann and wanting it, I tried it. Once I broke that barrier, I found that there was really no barrier at all."

Leaning forward in her chair, Ann reaches out to take Rick's hand. "I think most people are too closed in. I think everybody ought to try bisexuality. You should try everything once. If you don't like it, then don't do it again. If you like it, continue it. Don't let society dictate what you should or shouldn't like.

"You know, people pretend they like what they're doing even when they hate it. I have lots of friends, chicks, who would rather go out with other chicks, but they don't because they're supposed to go out with guys. My way of thinking is, do what you enjoy doing in sex, or if you don't enjoy sex, don't do it at all. There's no point to doing anything you don't want to. Life is to enjoy."

"Do you only do what you enjoy?"

Annoyed, she shakes her head. "Don't be silly and twist my words. I mean about sex. I don't enjoy working, but I have to do it. But there are plenty of optional things we do when we don't have to."

I look at Rick. "What about you, Rick? Have you a philosophy about bisexuality?"

He smiles at that. "That's a scary word, 'philosophy.' I guess I haven't been into it long enough to form a philosophy. I guess I eventually will. We all form philosophies on everything we do, if we keep doing it. But you can't really have an attitude about something you've only done five or six times. It hasn't changed what I feel about sex, or about life in general. I always was kind of free, and I did what I wanted to. I guess that was the Catholic school. I figured if I listened to them, hell, I wouldn't even have sex with a woman until I was married, and I knew that was wrong. So I figured everything else they said was wrong, like only having sex when you want a kid. Hell, that's plain ridiculous."

"Sex loosens you up," Ann cuts in. "It relaxes you. It puts you at ease. And yet most people who haven't had it are afraid of it, and there are some people who've never had it and still hate it, or people who have it but never enjoy it—and there are some people who have it and love it. I had a girl friend who was so up tight it was pathetic, but the moment she started screwing her whole attitude changed. She loosened up. She communicated with me eye to eye, instead of drifting around the room. She was a freer human being. Well, maybe if someone is able to screw both sexes, he's still freer. Do you know what I mean?"

"I think so, and that's why I asked about Rick. Do you think he's freer now?"

"He's loosened up. When he's with a guy, I see him more at ease. I see him that way with women, too—there are just more options."

Rick is smiling at her intensity, and I turn to him. "But you say you haven't sensed a change in yourself."

He laughs a little. "Well, I do crazy things now. I steal plants when I get drunk. I talk to pigeons—crazy things."

"He means he has fun now," Ann says, looking at him fondly.

"And the way you feel about Ann? Is that affected by your bisexuality?"

"Of course. I like everything about her—just the way she is with me, the way she treats me, and the concern that she has for me—just in general." He throws up his hands. "I like everything she does."

"How much of what you like is due to her bisexuality?"

"I liked her this way before, when I didn't know she was bisexual. I felt the same when I found out."

Earnestly, Ann says, "That's why I took him with me that first time, to watch. I wanted to make sure he wouldn't change."

"How did you feel about it?" I ask Rick.

"I was nervous. It was strange to me, but when I finally got into it myself, I said, now it's not so strange."

"Is Rick the first man you've had this close a relationship with?" I ask.

Ann considers. "There were other men, but not this close. Most men don't object to my bisexuality, but they won't try it. Their attitude was, 'You do it. Just don't tell me about it. Just leave Friday and Saturday night open for me.' But that's no good. It's better when you can be really honest."

I ask Rick, "Were there many girls before Ann?"

"Some—five or six."

"Does she give you something they didn't?"

Rick nods. "Yes, she does. She makes me feel closer to her than I ever did to anyone."

"Is it because of her bisexuality?"

"I really don't know," Rick says slowly. "I guess she'd treat me the same even if she weren't bisexual."

"Do you think you would?" I ask Ann.

She shrugs. "People who are bisexual are more open to new ideas and new ways to live. They'll try things. Straight people won't. You can't experiment with them. Rick and I can experiment and try new things. It's not a dead end. He's open about things. He'll consider them, think it over and then make a decision. Sexually straight people are more conservative, more closed in. You know, if you're open in sex, you're open in a lot of other things."

Ann has a point here and she tries to make it clearer, her forehead wrinkling as she talks, her face concerned and serious. "It isn't necessary that you do new things, that you practice bisexuality, just that you're open to the idea, that you don't condemn it. That's being open.

"Bisexuals are even more open. They not only consider it, they go out and do it. Now if someone won't try something you like, it stands to reason you won't be as open with them as with someone who will. That's really the secret of what Rick and I have."

We are all quiet for a moment, then I ask, "If you had kids, how would you feel about them?"

Ann looks at Rick, then smiles. "O.K. I'd want them to do what they wanted to do. I'd tell them my viewpoint, all I knew, and the possible consequences of what they did, but in the end I'd want them to do what they wanted to. Hell, it's their life. Anyway, I think they'd do it anyway, and I'd rather have them tell me they're going to.

"You know, if my parents had gone along with me I might still be with them, or at least in contact and friendly. They'd know what I was up to. They'd know where their daughter was, instead of shutting the door on me."

"Have they ever tried to reach you?"

"There's no way they can," she said flatly.

"Are you sorry about that?"

Ann folds her hands under her chin and looks down. After a long while she sighs. "I wish they had been open enough to let me decide what I wanted to do with my life, and then had stood by. It's not easy being on your own." She looks up with a quick smile as if regretting the brief moment of self-pity. "Anyway, I've got Rick."

I watch them leave the office later, holding hands, and I push back the chair and close the doors. Outside, they're standing at the entrance to the park and Rick is trying to coax a squirrel into eating out of his hand. I wave and walk down the block.

Rebellion takes many forms, and I believe the story of Ann and Rick is a typical saga of adolescent rebellion. Unfortunately, in our culture the word "rebellion" itself has a negative connotation. This negative feeling about rebellion is fairly well confined to adults, because they have often "grown up" and "sold out." The oldsters have long since forgotten their own early strivings against the restrictive and repressive measures of their own adult world and repressed or suppressed their strivings for a brave new world in order to accept the husk of a burned-out morality. We have forgotten America's two hundred years of positive fruits of rebellion against a myriad of repressions. We have forgotten that the heroes of yesterday were creatures of flesh and blood vilified and persecuted in their own times.

It's extremely difficult for us to look at our children and see heroic intent in their acts of rebellion. It's all too easy to view them as disobedient children who have not yet learned the ways of the world, who have not yet learned to fit in.

We say we want children who can think for themselves and grow up to be independent human beings, and yet we attempt on almost every hand to force them into our own mold—to force them into our way of thinking, or suffer our wrath and self-righteous rejection. Where is our toleration, our understanding, our democracy? A million children inhabit the streets as runaways, and many thousands are lost as useful productive members of society. Other thousands are raped, maimed, beaten, or killed. Such things are, obviously, much worse than not coming home at the prescribed hour or smoking. I wonder, if parents were given the choice, which they would take for their child?

Ann is running away from a rigid repressive home situation. She was not allowed to date boys, and this, for the normal teen-ager, is repressive. Her father was afraid of the sexual contacts Ann might have. It is not unnatural for a father to have a realistic concern about the possibility of his daughter being raped or becoming pregnant, but it is not natural to implement this concern by stopping all contact with the opposite sex. The least we could say is that there was little trust of Ann by her father.

Compounding this restrictive attitude on her father's part was the religion of her mother. This religion believes it is wrong to have sexual contact before marriage. Christian Science believes one must always have "right thoughts," and sexual thoughts are not "right." It is difficult for a teen-ager not to have sexual thoughts, so Ann constantly felt guilty and oppressed because of her mother's religious taboos about sex.

In addition, her mother's church does not believe in doctors or medicine. Year after year, Ann would have headaches and would have to suffer through them without medication. This was true whether she had a headache or an earache or something more serious.

On the other hand, her mother would violate her own religious principles and spank or hit Ann. This did very little to draw Ann close to either her religion or her mother. What it did accomplish was to make her feel unloved by her mother and begin a pattern of rebellion against authority.

Ann did not feel loved so she left her home in an attempt to find that love somewhere else. She has been constantly searching for it in a fairly undiscriminating manner.

In talking with Rick, I did not get the same feeling of rebellion as with Ann. The energy level was quite different. Rick was quiet, subdued, and slow. His intellect was no match for Ann's, whose mind worked with the rapidity of a machine gun and the precision of a well-oiled machine. His eyes were warm and his manner gentle.

There seems no question that Ann is the dominant partner in their relationship. Where she has definite opinions and well-thought-out intellectual positions, he tends to be an echo. It's not the echo of a parrot, but of a person in love who is attempting to please and to fit in.

There are many bisexuals who parade their sexual lives like a defiant banner as they ride into battle against what they consider to be the outmoded ramparts of society. This is not the case with Rick. He can take it or leave it. He is a man of the streets who has tested his manhood in back alleys, on the job, and in bed and found himself to be a man. One has the distinct impression that if something was to happen to his relationship with Ann, he would drop his bisexuality. He is strong enough within himself as a man so that he can go along with Ann's desires without feeling less of a man.

Both Ann and Rick place great stress on their desire to divorce themselves from the demands of society. They frequently mention the foolishness of conforming to the required norms of society. One reason they both give for engaging in bisexuality is wanting to do what is prohibited. Ann said, "You want what you're told you can't have." It is curious that, at the same time, they both seem extremely sensitive to the reactions of their peer group. They said it would surprise one to know how many people they met who are bisexual. It was important to them that their friends could accept their different sexual life. To be accepted by their friends made it all right.

I would raise the question of how much they have really shaken off the necessity for society's approval. It seems they have substituted one society for another—the younger for the older. In this sense, they are still seeking approval, but from a different set of people.

We are all familiar with the fads of the young. We know they are great imitators and tend to be swept along with the crowd, whether it be in terms of dress or lifestyle. If somewhere is the "in" place to go, hordes of people go there. If something is the "in" thing to do, there is a rush to do it. I believe this is just now beginning to happen with bisexual experimentation. The world "experimentation" is an appropriate one, because it seems to me that is what happens when a new trend begins to develop. The new trend appears and receives enough popular support to gain a minority of adherents. This support gains strength through coverage in newspapers, magazines, and TV. At this point, a certain number of people lose their fear and decide to experiment. They follow the old adage, "Don't knock it if you haven't tried it," or "Try it, you may like it." Bisexuality among the young seems to be just beginning to enter this phase of experimentation.

Rick and Ann, I believe, are typical of this experimental group. Rick did not want to be left out of the scene by Ann. It is almost as if he were willing to experiment with anything as long as it was an essential part of their relationship. I do not believe he would continue in his sexual relations with men if he broke up with Ann or if she went "straight."

Rick approaches his sexual relations with men as sexual encounters and not as relationships. This seems to be a critical distinction in the verbalizations made about bisexuality. Most discussions about the subject by those claiming to lead a bisexual life stress the necessity for relating to the "whole person" and not merely on a sexual basis. The homosexual man who is trying to also "get it on" with women will explain he is not simply looking for a one-night stand. He claims he does not want to hop from one bed partner to another. There always seems to be an attempt to relate on levels other than sex. Time is important. They feel it may happen that sex is brief, lasting only a time or two, but that this is only an accident along the way toward finding a lasting, fuller life with one person at a time.

It seems to me Ann and Rick are a couple whose commitment to bisexuality is temporary. Ann, in a state of rebellion, is in an active state of experimentation, and Rick follows along, feeling somehow it will all pass.

9

Dan

Dan's apartment is in a better part of Greenwich Village, the rear half of a second floor in a brownstone. It's one big room with the back windows overlooking a garden, but he's used some surprising tricks to make it livable. The bed is on a sleeping loft built over the kitchen and bathroom. A black, upright piano and hi-fi equipment are on a raised platform backing on the windows. The ceiling is high, and one wall has a wood-burning fireplace flanked by a modern white leather couch and two leather-and-chrome chairs. The pictures are modern and good, the shelves along one wall filled with books—the total effect smart and sophisticated, and surprisingly neat and clean.

Dan offers me a drink, and I settle for a glass of wine and sink down on the couch where one of three Siamese cats immediately leaps onto my lap and makes himself comfortable.

I'm impressed with the room, and Dan accepts my admiration. "I like to live comfortably." He stretches out on the other end of the couch and puts the wine bottle on the coffee table. "I couldn't afford to have it done professionally, so I built all of this myself. I've never been one to compromise."

Dan is in his late twenties, short and compact, his tanned body showing the results of some extensive weightlifting. He has a black beard and moustache, and he wears skintight jeans with a broad belt and a studded buckle. His T-shirt is short of his belt by three inches and the sleeves have been cut off at the shoulders. On his left wrist there's a wide leather-and-metal wristband.

I ask him what he means by compromise.

"When I like something, I go after it. I don't settle for second best. I wanted this room to look luxurious, like something out of the movies, and that's the effect I got."

"Do you feel that way about the rest of your life?"

"Yes. When I want a thing I go after it—hard. I was like that when I was a kid. I wanted to play the piano, and I kept at it night and day. I never had to be coaxed to practice. I wanted to be more than good at it. I wanted to be the best!"

I look at the piano and ask, "Do you still play?"

"I play for a living. I work at a Village club, but I still practice every day."

"What are you into?"

"Rock. I play jazz piano, too." He nods at the black lacquered piano. "I brought that here from Detroit. But I still play classical stuff, I still practice my classical music."

"Is that where you grew up, Detroit?"

"Yeah. Grammar school, high school, and college, and I lived at home all the way."

"What was it like?"

"Detroit?" He considers. "Not really bad. I had a good

time as a kid, and college was a ball. I think I would have
stayed in Detroit if it hadn't been for my music."

"How do you mean?"

He shrugs. "New York's where it's at, as far as music goes.
I did some college shows and got an offer to come East on
an off-Broadway deal."

"You make it sound very easy and quick. How did you
get started in music?"

He frowns. "I was always interested in music. Before she
was married, my mother sang in an opera company here in
New York. She never forgot it." There is pride mixed with
humor in his voice. "And she never let us forget it either.
I remember her doing the housework and singing arias from
Puccini, and drowning out the vacuum cleaner with Wag-
ner."

"What was she, musically?"

"A mezzo-soprano—with balls. She could really belt it
out." He shakes his head admiringly. "There was always
music around the house. Mom loved music. She always en-
couraged me to play, and when I began to compose she
couldn't do enough to help me out. She was always taking
me to concerts." He smiles gently. "Some of my greatest
memories are rainy afternoons when I'd sit on the floor
listening to records with Mom, hearing her sing along with
the music and knowing her voice was better than any of
the stars on the records."

"When was the first time your music was recognized in
public? When was it first played?"

"When I was fourteen. I wrote a musical score for our
church operetta. Mom was so proud she made me play the
music for everyone who came to the house. It drove my
father crazy." His voice flattens, losing its soft quality of
reminiscence.

"He wasn't around much, and when he was I don't think
he ever listened. If he had to be there, he'd bury himself in
a book or the paper. Mom used to nag him all the time.

She'd complain, 'I could have had a great career if I hadn't gotten married. I was right up there.' You know, a lot of people say that, but with Mom it was really true. She had reached the top in New York. And it wasn't just that she could sing well, but it was the feeling she had for music. It was tremendous, like the feeling she had for everything in life, full of gusto and eagerness. There wasn't anything in town she wasn't involved in. Some people called her a club woman, but she was more than that. She was a real leader in the community. She was on every committee for every worthwhile cause." His voice is very intense, very eager to convince me.

"What is she doing now?"

Dan's words are suddenly soft and quiet. "She died five years ago."

"I'm sorry."

"It was a terrible thing because she was still so young. She had so much to live for." His voice breaks.

"You sound as if you took her death very hard."

"I did. I just fell apart when she died. I couldn't do anything. I had to drop out of school. I think that's what caused me to develop a stomach ulcer, at least the doctor said so. Even now, talking about it, I can feel my stomach knot up."

"How did your father take her death?"

"Worse than I did. It's funny, because I never thought they were very close. She was always giving him a hard time, and he was never really involved with our family life, but we had to put him in a sanatorium under the care of a psychiatrist. It was hard on him because, you know, he was a doctor, a G.P., and he always worried about what his colleagues would say."

Curious, I ask, "Why do you think it hit him so hard?"

"I've thought a lot about that. Maybe because Mom did so much for him, and he never really let her know whether or not he appreciated it. Mom devoted most of her life to the family—too bad it wasn't the other way around."

"What do you mean?"

"Well, Dad's only interest was medicine. That was his whole world. When I was a kid I rarely saw him. Even when he made plans to go out with us, say on a picnic, some patient would call at the last minute and he'd cancel everything and rush off on a house call. Mom and I always felt we were afterthoughts. You know, most kids remember doing something special with their fathers, playing ball or going swimming—not me! He never had time. He just didn't like to do any of the things I thought were fun. In fact, he always put them down. He always said nothing was really important except medicine."

"Did he ever help your mother?"

"Help? Dad? You've got to be kidding. I never saw him lift a finger around the house. Mom worked herself to death. Oh, we always had a live-in housekeeper, but Mom made all the decisions and ran the house. Sometimes it seemed as if my Dad was a paying guest in the house, for all the time he was there. As a kid I used to wonder why she married him. He was very wealthy. Not only his practice, but he had inherited money and invested it well. He could afford anything he wanted, and one thing you have to say in his favor, he was very generous with his money. I had anything I wanted, more clothes and toys than any kid on the block. When I got into music I had the best instruments and teacher in town." He bites his lip. "Shit, I'd have given every bit of it to keep him home more. That's all I ever wanted, him, not the lousy money!"

"Who ran the family?"

"There was never any question about that. It was Mom. Dad never bothered to make a decision outside of his practice. Mom chose the furniture, decided where we'd live, where we'd go on vacation—and then, when we got to go, Dad somehow never made it. There was always some emergency problem. But Mom never let that get in our way. We went anyway. Mom and me. We used to joke about it, though we were both hurt." He laughs. "Mom used to tease me about being her date, and you know, I liked it when people stared at us, wondering what an older woman was doing out with a young kid. We flirted and acted as if we were both dating, just to get a rise out of everyone. Sometimes we even held hands."

I look around the apartment. "You're living pretty well here. Your father must be helping you. Are you any closer to him now?"

"No way. Don't let this place fool you. I told you I did it all myself. I sweated blood putting up the felt and building that bed platform, and Dad never gave me a cent to live on. He told me, you leave Detroit, you do it on your own. Well, I did. All on my own. I support myself. Maybe I have some rough times, but I pull down a good salary in the clubs, and some big groups have used my stuff. I get by."

"You still don't get along with him?"

"Dad? He doesn't get along with me. As soon as I left college he cut me off. He figured, if I didn't make M.D., what was the use of having anything to do with me."

"He didn't like the idea of music as a profession?"

Dan laughs. "You better believe he didn't." He imitates his father's voice, very pompous, very didactic. "Music is not a serious thing to do with your life. You'll end up penniless without a profession." He drops the mimicry. "Maybe it reminded him of my mother. I don't know. At any rate, he sure never helped me out."

"Were you bisexual back in Detroit?"

"No way. I wasn't even sure what it meant. I began making it with girls when I was still in high school, and in college there was a lot of sexual activity through the frats. That's how I got my first case of gonorrhea."

"How did that happen?"

"Some girl they brought in to service the whole house."

Stretching out, he puts his feet on the coffee table. "I was
one of twenty guys who came down with it."

"Did it bother you?"

"Bother me! It absolutely destroyed me. I couldn't believe
it. I always thought only degenerates and the royal families
got gonorrhea. I also thought it would ruin me, that I'd
never be able to have kids. I was terrified, too, at the idea
of seeing a doctor."

"But you did?"

"The health department came to see us, and gave us a
few shots of penicillin and that was it. But I just couldn't
believe I was cured. For a year afterward I was afraid to
touch a girl, and when I finally did, I was impotent. Christ,
it was a bad trip, really bad." He sighs. "I got over it eventually, but it sure took the edge off sex."

"Did your parents find out?"

"No. I was scared as hell that Dad would know, and
when I went home I avoided even talking to him. I was
sure with his medical knowledge he'd spot it immediately,
I don't know how, but I was sure he would. But I didn't
have to worry. He never bothered to talk to me. I don't
even think he know I was home, he was so involved with
his office."

"When did you have your first homosexual experience?"

"At a party here in the Village. We were both pretty high,
and we left together. He asked me if I was interested, and I
started to say no, then decided, what the hell. I'd give it
a try."

"How did it go?"

Frowning a litle, he scratches his beard. "I enjoyed it,
but I didn't really groove on it. It was just something that
happened."

"As casually as that?" I ask dubiously.

"Oh, well, I guess I must have been thinking about it for
a while before that or I'd never have said yes." He looks
thoughtful. "When I moved here from Detroit, I began to

get involved with a pretty sophisticated crowd, the bunch who were doing my off-Broadway musical. Most of the guys in the cast were gay or swung both ways, and after working with them I began to accept the possibility of it."

"For yourself?"

"No, not at first. Actually, I was frightened about it. I thought, if I let it, it could destroy my manhood."

"Destroy? In what way?"

"Oh, I don't know. I was very involved with being a man, with looking and acting masculine, tough. That was when I grew my beard, and I hung around with a motorcycle gang here in the Village. It gave me a sense of being physically tough. I took up weightlifting too."

"Why do you think you felt the need for all that?"

Thoughtfully, he says, "Maybe it was my music. Back in Detroit, in school, the kids equated music with being sissyish. Here it was different. The rock groups had changed all that, but I still had this uneasiness about my music."

"Yet you wouldn't give it up."

He laughs. "I'd sooner give up masculinity! No, I wanted both. I wanted my music and I wanted to be a man."

"Are you still concerned about your manhood?"

"No—" He hesitates. "Although in a funny way I still enjoy maleness, toughness. The guys I have affairs with have to be real men—hard physically. But I think I began to lose the fear about my manhood after seeing so much homosexuality all around me. I made some good friends in the show, and they were all gay, so what the hell—I learned it's the man underneath that counts. Superficial things like appearance and sexual persuasion don't matter."

"And after that party you had your first affair. How long had you been in New York?"

"Oh, about two and a half years."

"And that was the first man you had sex with. How did you react?"

"Scared. I had trouble turning on, but I enjoyed it," he

adds quickly, defensively. "I didn't hear from him for a while after that, even though we exchanged numbers. I wouldn't make the next move. I waited him out, and he finally called me after two weeks. Then we had supper together and talked a little about it. I think he was more curious about my reaction than I was about his."

"What was your reaction?"

He frowns at that, twisting his leather armband. "I didn't feel that he had seduced me, brought me out. It wasn't that type of thing. Hell, in the two weeks since we were together, I kept having sex with girls. When we talked that night at supper, I remember telling him that it was something I could deal with, and it was. I had no intention of giving up girls, but I was willing to go to bed with him again."

"Did you?"

"Yeah. A few times. I liked him and I didn't think of him as gay, just a guy I liked enough to have sex with. I wanted to see if it was easier a second time, and it was. I turned on more, and when I wasn't with him I thought about him. But I still would have taken a girl if I had a choice. After that I began to get curious. I'd lived in the Village since I'd come to New York, and I knew about the gay bars, but I'd never been inside one. I was actually afraid to, but he agreed to go in with me and I felt more secure."

"How do you mean, secure?"

He frowns, moving uneasily. "I guess I felt threatened by a bar full of homosexual men."

"Threatened? How?"

"Well—it's hard to explain. I wasn't afraid of them—I've never really met a gay guy who was that aggressive, who wouldn't stop if I made it clear that I wasn't interested, but I think I was a little afraid of myself, of my own reactions."

"What were your reactions?"

He shakes his head. "Confused, I guess. I was attracted and repelled." He hesitates. "I suppose I was afraid of the attraction, afraid to let myself go. Anyway, my friend and I started going to the gay bars together. They were bars he liked, but I didn't."

"Why not?"

"Well—" He considers, then grimaces. "They tended to be a little on the Nellie side, you know, men dancing with men. That's a turn-off to me."

"Why?"

"That type of man just doesn't attract me. When I want a man, I want a man, not a man pretending to be a woman."

"What do you feel about those men?"

"I get angry at them."

"Angry? Why?"

"Well—it's a little like looking in a mirror and seeing myself, and not a flattering reflection. Do you know what I mean?"

"I'm not sure I do."

"Well, look. There's obviously some gay element in me. I know that because I can react to other men. O.K., if I'm like that, then I resemble other gay men. If those men are distasteful to me, then I'm distasteful to myself."

"Are you trying to say you identify with gay men, and want their image to be something you aren't ashamed of?"

"Exactly." He seems relieved at the way I've put it. "That's just what I mean, and that's why I get sore as hell at the mincing guys. To tell the truth, I'd like to take a swing at them."

"Have you ever done that?"

He's silent for a while, then, grudgingly, he says, "Yes. I've been in a few fights with fags where I've beaten them up."

"And did you enjoy it?"

Again the silence, then, reluctantly, "Yes. Yes, I did enjoy it, but it scared me, too. I don't like to lose control of myself."

"Did you?"

"In a way. Look, I'd rather not talk about it."

Changing the subject, I ask, "Do you feel that the male body is more stimulating, sexually, than the female?"

"I wouldn't say that. It's stimulating in a different way."

"In what way?"

"It's a different sensation to touch a male body, and to be touched by one."

"What type of man attracts you?"

Again he fingers his wristband. "A very masculine man, butch. The kind you might meet at an S-and-M leather bar. Incidentally, those are the bars I like to go to."

His eyes move down his own tight-fitting jeans, his boots and belt, and I have a momentary impression of sexual self-approval. "What does the leather wristband signify?" I ask.

"Nothing. It's just something I like to wear. Even when I was a kid I always wore butch clothes, Levis and a flannel shirt, but it doesn't signify anything to me except the fact that I like to wear them—I like the look of them."

I sense some discomfort in this area, and I move away. "But with all the leather and butch clothes, you still continue your heterosexual life."

"A lot of people your age make the mistake of equating the way you dress with the way you live. O.K., now I like to dress like this, but if I were going to a classical concert, for instance, I'd wear what's called for."

"And tonight calls for jeans and T-shirt?"

He looks at me quickly to see if I'm putting him down, then he shrugs. "I didn't know what you were like."

"But you knew someone older was interviewing you?"

"You might be bisexual—or gay. How could I tell?"

I agree and smile, and he smiles back, then pours himself another glass of wine. "You know, I don't put other men in any different role than I put myself. Hell, you can like ice cream and not prefer chocolate to vanilla."

I nod. "That's true, of course. But if you had your choice, which would you take?"

"Ice cream? Maybe chocolate." He laughs. "I don't know.
It has to depend on the mood I'm in."

"And with people, would you take men or women?"

"It's pretty fifty-fifty. I can go one week balling with guys
and the next balling with girls. It really depends on the
frame of mind I'm in. Too many people live programmed
lives. Up at eight, work from nine to five, then home to
another routine. Me, I like to stay as unplanned as possible.
As a matter of fact, I find it almost impossible to make long-
range plans, and the same goes for men and women. I think
whichever fits my frame of mind at the minute is the one
for me."

"How do you get any stability in your life that way?"

"I'm not so sure stability is all that good. If you have to
sacrifice pleasure for stability, I don't think you're all that
much ahead. What the hell, no one knows how long he'll be
around. I may be here today and gone tomorrow. While I'm
here I want to enjoy life."

Seeing a contradiction, I say, "And yet you tell me that
you're very disciplined about your music, that you still spend
hours practicing, that you always did."

He brushes that aside. "Oh well—I enjoy that. I love my
music. I don't look on that as stability."

"But it is. You can be stable when you enjoy something,
when you want something."

He's silent for a while. Then he nods. "I guess, if I thought
it through I'd have to admit that music is the exception. I'll
work my balls off to amount to something in the field—but
I don't look at it as sacrifice or work, even if it is. That's the
point. It's what I want to do, what gives me pleasure."

"But, by the same token, if you met a woman you really
wanted to live with, would you sacrifice your relationships
with men?"

"Why should I?"

"Suppose it was the only way you could hold on to her."

"Well—if I really wanted her, I guess I would. If I want

something, I'll do a hell of a lot to get it. Maybe what it boils down to is that I haven't wanted any man or woman that much."

"But you have wanted music?"

"Yes, and I work at it. I play in a Village nightclub three nights a week, and in another coffee house the other nights. I work with an off-Broadway group, and I put out a hell of a lot of stuff. It's not all good, but some of it is."

"Do you have serious relationships with any women?"

He stands up and walks to the window, pulling the blinds aside for a moment, then turns to face me, his fingers looped in his belt.

"Of course I have. I've got one going on right now, but I've also had some deep relationships with men. I don't have any now."

"Have you had any at the same time?"

"With a man and a girl?"

"Yes."

"Sure."

"When you're into something like that," I ask carefully, "a fairly heavy relationship with both, what do you feel in terms of fidelity?"

"Fidelity?" He sounds surprised.

"Yes. Faithfulness. Do you feel you want to be faithful to either one?"

He strides to the chair opposite me and throws himself down, looping one leg over the arm. "I don't believe in sexual faithfulness. Even if I were married in the conventional sense, I wouldn't be monogamous. I couldn't stay faithful to one person. Look, sometimes sex can have everything to do wtih love, and sometimes it has absolutely nothing to do with it. It can be a pure physical release and outlet. I enjoy attractive people and interesting people, and I like to know them physically, too, sexually."

"I don't think I quite understand that." I frown.

"Look, how many people do you know who are faithful? Most men aren't, and I bet those who are wish they weren't and dream about outside sex. If you could assure them they'd never be caught, how many would refuse an affair? Me, I'm just more honest. I'm telling you the way it is, not the way you think it should be." Scratching his beard, he says, "I also find that in terms of my music, experiencing a lot of people physically gives me a better insight into things."

"How do you mean?"

"I get to know more of life, a greater variety of life. I can judge people better. In the intimacy of a sexual relationship you get to know how people act and react, and that helps in composing. It helps in any creative process, but it particularly helps me in music."

"Tell me how."

He spreads his arms, smiling. "Well, it's hard to explain, but say I'm performing and I have to judge the reaction of the audience. I have to know people to do that. I have to know how they think, how all different people, men as well women, think and react."

"And you can get that from sexual encounters?" I ask doubtfully.

"Not sexual alone. Every sexual encounter is an encounter with a person, with another human. You learn how people react and think, what turns them on. When I'm composing something I know what moves me. If I know my relationship to other people, then I know what moves them, too. It's like an equation."

"What's the unknown factor?"

He smiles. "People. And you solve the equation when you solve people. Do you see?"

"Not completely. It seems to me you could learn all that if you stuck to one person sexually and knew a variety of people socially."

"No. Not me. I don't know a person until I know them sexually. I don't really know them until then."

"And you couldn't see yourself settling down with one person?"

He smiles. "Not right now, but, you know, people change. I'm not saying that in two years or even in two weeks I might not find the one person I'd like to be with all the time. But it's not something I want to do right now."

"Could you see yourself getting into a purely homosexual or heterosexual relationship?"

He purses his lips and considers. "Maybe. With all my feeling against faithfulness, I still might. As I said, people change. A lot of my friends are living together, and they never thought they would. It might happen to me, but right now I consider myself loose in my relationships, not locked into anything. I'm concerned with satisfying my partner, whoever it is, and with being satisfied myself." Smugly, he adds, "And I'm pretty good at both."

"Do you mean you're more sensual than other people?"

"And better sexually."

"Is it determining what your partner likes and supplying it?"

"Well, yes, in a way. I get a lot of pleasure out of satisfying my partner. That makes me feel, well, more competent. I feel very strongly that sex must be enjoyed by both partners. That's why so many marriages break up. The gal rolls over and asks for sex. A lot of women tell me their husbands put it in, pop off, roll over, and go to sleep. That's not sex. That's putting down the woman. I want to go into sex as an equal, and that means I have to find out what the woman—or man—wants and enjoys." He's quiet, twisting his wristband, then he looks up at me and his defiance and "tough" attitude is gone and he seems very young, very defenseless. "If my parents had understood that, things wouldn't have been so goddamned difficult."

"How do you mean?"

"If they could have shared life, if Mom had been interested in his medical practice—like maybe running his office, involving herself with his interest instead of hating it so—or if he had tried to understand her music and had given her some help with it, things would have been different." His voice has a yearning note. "We could have had so much fun—such good times—if they really cared about each other and shared things."

"Do you think they shared things sexually?"

Bitterly, he says, "I know they didn't. They wouldn't have been at each other all the time if they had." He shrugs. "Maybe that's why I haven't a long-term thing with a guy or gal. Maybe I'm afraid it'll turn into what they had. To tell you the truth, I'd rather have a quick affair without too much involvement."

"Have there been many quick pickups in your homosexual affairs?"

He shifts a bit uncomfortably. "Yes. I can get into a situation, like getting on a subway car and having a guy turn on to me and then going home with him."

"Does it happen often?"

"Occasionally. If the other guy is groovy-looking. Hell, in that kind of sex there's very little contact. I've seen even quicker sex going on in subway johns, but that's not my scene."

"How about cruising on the streets?"

"Well, sometimes, but that kind of sex is a whole different thing."

"What do you mean by 'that kind of sex'?"

"I mean when you go out looking and don't really care what you find, when all you want is the physical act and you don't want to know the guy, his name even. That degrades the whole sexual act. It's like paying for a prostitute. You can't think much of yourself if you do it."

Two of the Siamese cats start a scuffle near the piano, and in a sudden flash of anger Dan sends them scampering. Then, with an apologetic smile, he returns. "Can I get you something else?"

"This is fine." I pour some wine and ask, "How would you contrast this quick sex with something that develops slowly, where you get to know the other person first?"

Frowning, he says, "That's very hard to do, get to know the other person when it's homosexual sex. It's hard to build up a relationship first and then get into a sexual situation. It's almost impossible."

Puzzled, I ask, "Why?"

"Well—" He spreads his hands. "Almost always, the first encounter is a sexual one, then you may get to know the guy. That's the nature of the gay scene. I know gay guys who go down to the bars every single night, and if they're lucky they may make out four out of seven times, and if they enjoy it once they're lucky. It's different with a woman. If I were working in an office and met a woman I found attractive, maybe I'd ask her out to dinner, take her to a movie, get to know her first before I let it get sexual, and most women wouldn't be annoyed by that. They'd think it normal. If they found me attractive and I let them know there was a sexual interest, they'd probably be content to wait.

"But men aren't like that, at least not the men I meet and the ones I'm attracted to. If I suggested to one that we have dinner together before we went to bed, he'd look at me as if I were out of my mind. You know, there are nights when I work late at the piano and get all tied up, and then I just want to go out and have a couple of beers or some-thing—I'm not really interested in sex, just in going out, and I enjoy the gay bars as much as the straight bars—but in a situation like that, if I walk in and start talking to someone, and he says, 'Do you want to leave?' and I say, 'I'm not really into anything tonight,' his reaction is, 'Why have you been wasting my time by talking to me for half an hour?' "

He stretches and stands up again, walking to the window to look down at the street. Again, in the way he moves, I am aware of the compact, muscular quality of his body. Turning to me, he says, "I don't blame this on the people as much as on the world. This is the reason gay bars exist, to meet other men to fuck—and that's basically what goes on there. I mean, I've met some men I've become friendly with, but most of them are men I've also balled."

"Do you ever see these quick pickups for a second or third time?"

"Oh, sure. On a sexual level and on a social level. I mean, there are guys I've made it with who are just great guys, and we stay friends without the sex, but by the same token there are women I make it with, and if after one or two times I'm not there anymore, I'll say, 'Look, I really like you. I'd like to get into your head. We've got things in common to share. Let's be friends.' And sometimes it works out." He smiles ruefully. "And sometimes it doesn't. There are men and women who want only a sexual relationship."

"I thought you were stressing the big difference between the homosexual and heterosexual approach."

"Well, yes, but some things are the same. Look. I can go down to the Buffalo Roadhouse, which is a mixed bar. It's primarily straights, but there are gay people there, so it's called mixed. I can be standing there with a group of friends and meet a chick, bring her back here and we'll start balling. You see, I'm not saying that immediate sexual contact isn't found in heterosexual relationships. What I'm saying is, if it doesn't happen, you don't immediately reject the partner. In a homosexual relationship, if there isn't instant sex, you figure something is wrong."

"Has the fact that you're bisexual affected the way you relate to women?"

He considers that for a moment and then shakes his head. "No, or only in the sense that it gives me another choice. It's made me aware that there's something out there besides women." He gestures at the window. "I've come to understand that given the chance, and given the freedom, one can be as good as the other—and there doesn't have to be a lot of trauma connected with it."

"Do you find that knowing men sexually affects your sexuality with women?"

"How do you mean?"

"Some women have told me they'd rather have a love affair with a bisexual man because he understands them better, he's more empathic and because he understands them better physically, how they respond to lovemaking."

One of the cats comes close, but when I reach for it, it slips away. Dan gestures, and it leaps to his lap. Stroking it, he says, "I think that what they're getting at is that once you, as a man, have made it with a guy, any male mystique you have about yourself is—well, not shattered, but in many areas you realize how false it is. You're able to do without it."

Looking at his leather-and-jeans outfit, I ask, "Do you consider yourself without the male mystique?"

"Don't let my clothes fool you. There's a difference between dressing up and the male mystique."

"What difference?"

"I dress up because I want to project an image. I like men who dress like this, and I think they like me when I dress this way. It's acting a role to let other know what I am—what I like. But the male mystique, the machismo crap, that's different. I don't have that and I don't need it. I'm a man, and I know it. I can function like a man—if a man functions any different from a woman. I build things. I like sports—what the hell is a man?"

I shake my head, looking around the room and admiring

the work he's put into it. "Did you do all this yourself?"
I ask.

"I'm good with my hands." Walking to the piano, he runs
his fingers over the keyboard. "Maybe that's a male trait,
though I know a lot of women who are good at this stuff.
A woman helped me rebuild this piano. Actually, I don't
have much time to fool around with this stuff anymore."

"Why not? What do you do with your time?"

"Are you kidding? Do you think composing is a nothing
job? Maybe I'm not on a nine to five schedule, but I do a
hell of a lot more than eight hours of work a day. I'm at
the club at night from eight until two in the morning. I
practice every day. I spend at least three hours a day composing—believe me, I put in more than a full day."

I test the piano awkwardly, and ask, "Is there such a
thing as a bisexual underground? I know homosexuals have
their own places. Is there an equivalent for bisexuals?"

He shrugs. "I don't know. Living down here, I go to
Village bars, mostly mixed bars."

"Gay men and women?"

"No gay and straight. The lesbians usually stick to themselves. Even in terms of sex, they want very little to do with
men. Some of them are beginning to come over and join
the gay organizations, but for a while, when they were
getting their consciousness raised, they didn't want anything
at all to do with men."

"So you don't know of any bisexual bars?"

"Well, there are a couple I've heard of where nothing is
labeled, but they are bisexual. At least the people who go
there have a certain sense of freedom about sexuality. You
do what you please and no one cares. You can't do that in
either straight bars or a gay bar." He smiles. "But you know,
by the same token I've been up to Maxwell's Plum, that big
swinging singles' bar in the east Sixties, and I've picked up
guys there. It depends on who is there at any one given

time. I've been up to Maxwell's with chicks and seen guys cruising guys."

"Are you trying to say the distinctions are falling away?"

"The distinctions are becoming less of an issue. Look, I prefer butch clothes and butch guys, but I like other men, too. If I see a guy and I'm attracted to him, and he to me, well—"

"Do you prefer a bisexual man or a homosexual one?"

"Most men I make it with are homosexual, but that's because there are more homosexuals than bisexuals. But I meet more and more guys in the homosexual community who dig women, too, and they're beginning to explore that about themselves."

"Do you think this bisexual trend is a passing thing or will it stay around for a while?"

"I don't think it's a passing thing. It's been around for a long time, but it's been in hiding. Homosexuality is coming out into the open now, and so is bisexuality. In general, people aren't as judgmental about sex these days."

"Speaking about sex being out in the open, does your father know about your bisexuality?"

"Yes, but his reaction was just like his reaction to everything else about me. He just withdrew and refused to talk about it."

"He didn't say anything at all?"

"A little, but it was all practical stuff. What would my friends say? What would the family say? What if his patients found out? How would it affect my getting a job? He never got into my feelings about it, what it meant to me in terms of personal happiness, but I expected that from him."

"How do the women you go with feel about your bisexuality, or do they know?"

Shrugging, he says, "If I'm carrying on a relationship with them, they can't help but know. With some I've gotten into some heavy discussions about it."

"What kind of discussions?"

Dan walks around the room as he talks now, and I get a sense of restlessness, a need to get out and away. "They want to know how men compare to them, and some get pretty up tight about it. But there are always a few who dig going to bed with a bisexual. It turns them on." He stops by the piano and touches a few chords tentatively. "There are also some who feel threatened by it. They feel there's just no way they can compete with a guy, and it's true—any more than a guy can compete with a girl. They're different. I've had homosexual friends who just stopped seeing me once they found out I went with girls, too."

I finish my wine and refuse his offer of more. "Tell me," I ask, "is there any point in competing?"

"Well, people have feelings and there's always human nature. In any relationship there's an element of jealousy."

He considers that as we walk to the door. "I think you find less, but only because there are many bisexuals who are more honest about sexual pleasure as opposed to relationships."

Looking at his watch, he decides it's still early enough to drop into a bar, so he comes downstairs with me. On the way, he says, "I think many heterosexuals are still caught up in the whole thing of what being faithful means. Me, I believe that if I love you, or if I'm having a thing with you, emotional or sexual or both, it doesn't mean I'm chained to you. I'm free and you're free—that's the whole point."

Although Dan claims to be bisexual in his actions, I get very little feeling that he has any basic attraction to women. People in the gay movement would say Dan is basically homosexual but will not admit it at this moment because it is too threatening to him. In this case, I would agree with them. It seems to me that all his discussions about women come as afterthoughts.

In psychological terms, we often speak of an unresolved homosexual conflict in people. This means that a person has a certain attraction to the same sex, but is not aware of its existence at any conscious level. Whenever this unconscious feeling comes close to the surface, every effort is made to repress it because it is too threatening. This attempt at repression can occur in an outburst or it can occur over a period of time. When it comes as an outburst, it usually takes the form of a strong denial of, or hostility against, homosexuals. One often sees this at a bar where a man makes a sexual advance to another man and receives some type of brutal response for his advances. The man with the unresolved homosexual conflict usually reacts violently toward any advance, because to react to it with a simple denial of the advance is not strong enough to handle the hidden homosexual drive. At the extreme, a fight might ensue after the advance in an effort to prove that homosexuals are weak and that the person who has been approached is a "real" man.

In cases where the denial takes place over a period of time, we see certain fairly standard actions. The person with the unresolved homosexual conflict will engage in various types of body-building exercises aimed at keeping him in perfect physical shape. This is not to say that everyone who does physical exercises has an underlying unresolved homosexual conflict. We have to look at the way he goes about the exercises—the intensity involved in keeping in excellent physical condition. There is usually a do-or-die feeling about the exercises.

Dan denies the way he dresses has anything to do with his homosexual side. Objectively, this might be true, but it is not so with Dan. His dress is another attempt to show to the world, and, more importantly, to himself, that he is not a homosexual. The leather wristband and the overemphasis on "butch" dress is an effort to combat the feminine side he feels within himself. It is like a painting in which we have to take into consideration all the various colors in order to see the total picture. Dan's clothes, plus his intensity about exercises and being in perfect physical shape, blend together to paint a picture of the homosexual.

We can take this interpretation a little further. Dan makes a strong point of relating to men who are "real" men. There is a necessity within him to identify only with those characteristics that are culturally associated with maleness. If he were attracted to anything regarded by our society as feminine, he would run the risk of having to look at his homosexual side, which would be threatening.

Dan also has a strong desire to be in control. He appears to lead the way in all his relationships. Again we cannot isolate this part of a person's personality and attribute the entire personality structure to that element. On the other hand, we cannot overlook it when it forms part of the larger picture. If Dan were to let things get out of control, he would also run the danger of having his feminine side emerge. Culturally, we associate passivity with being feminine. This is certainly not true objectively, but one tends to act upon culturally accepted norms rather than objective truths. In listening to Dan, one gets the strong feeling that he would feel very uncomfortable if he were not "running the show."

In attempting to get any insights into what made Dan the way he is today, at least in his homosexual side, we face a complicated problem. It is essentially the problem of what factors go into forming a homosexual pattern.

The first question one has to resolve in thinking about the causal factors in homosexual activity is that of heredity versus environment. There are many professionals in the field of psychology and psychiatry who believe homosexuality is genetic, therefore not subject to change. On the other extreme are those who feel it is entirely determined by how the child was raised by his parents. Whichever side one chooses, all reasoning follows from this first decision.

I believe one has to keep an open mind on the question

because we do not have enough solid evidence in the study of homosexuals to form a definite conclusion. However, I lean heavily to the environmental side.

When we look at the childhood of many homosexuals, we see a certain type of family situation. It is usually described as a weak father and a dominating or excessively strong mother. A strong attachment is built up between the mother and son in which the son identifies with the characteristics of the mother. He cannot identify with the weak father. If the identification is *complete,* we see a full-fledged homosexual emerge, but if it is not, we tend to see the outside trappings of a homosexual or of a "strong/controlling/masculine" person.

This pattern is present in an almost classical manner in Dan. His father never had time for him and was completely engrossed in the practice of medicine. On top of this, the father appeared to Dan to be incapable of making decisions outside his professional office. In other words, in culturally acceptable terms he was not a "real man." Not only did his father not have time for the usual father-son games and sports, but he didn't even have time to talk to him. One is forced to say that there was almost no male figure for Dan to identify with.

His mother, on the other hand, presented a picture he could identify with easily. She paid attention to him and made every effort to help him with his music. She took long hours out of her community activities and housework, devoting them to being with her son. Again we cannot say this is "abnormal" in itself, or we would run the risk of saying that too many mothers are in danger of creating homosexual children. We must look at it in the larger context of the family situation. Dan's mother was a very strong person, and in reality, she took over both the male and female roles in the family. Dan could get both male and female identification in one person.

This type of identification, unfortunately, seems to lead to a great confusion in the mind and feelings of the child. I get the impression that Dan and his mother were almost lovers. The words and feelings with which he describes his mother are usually reserved for lovers. If Dan had any early childhood sexual feelings toward his mother, they would certainly have had to be pushed down quickly and violently denied. In later life this leads to a certain difficulty in relating sexually to any woman, because she runs the danger of being associated with mother.

Dan's family was certainly not a marriage model for him to follow. It would be very difficult for Dan to see the man getting anything out of marriage if he looked at the life of his father. His father said to him in so many words that the only important thing in one's life is his profession. No wonder Dan says many times that he has never really gotten involved with a sexual partner and that his music is the most important thing in his life.

I would predict it would not be too long before Dan gives up any pretense of dealing with women and settles into a standard homosexual life. At the present he is living through a bisexual phase, but I think it is simply a phase.

10
Ellis and Linda

Ellis McCarthy and his wife, Linda, live in Newton, a suburb of Boston. Their house is on a quiet tree-shaded street. It is white clapboard, newly built, but with an old New England feel to it. We sit out back in a pleasant, fenced-in yard surrounded by brilliant flower beds. Ellis nods at the flowers. "They're all Linda's. She has this crazy touch with flowers. She says it's a matter of vibes, but I suspect it's her fertilizer. She's a farm girl at heart."

"Where is she from?"

"New York State, the Finger Lakes region. Her parents have a farm there, and Linda takes the kids there for most of the summer."

"And you're a summer bachelor."

"I can't get more than two weeks off." He shrugs. "I'm still a junior partner in the law firm. But I do well. We manage some pretty big foundations, and I like it. I don't mind spending most of the summer alone. It gives me time to find myself."

"Find yourself? In what way?"

Ellis scratches his head. He's a tall, rangy man with an unruly shock of grayish red hair, a sandy, drooping mustache, and a reddish, freckled complexion. "Maybe find myself isn't the right way of putting it. Know myself, maybe. I want to get in touch with whatever's inside me."

"How do you go about it?"

He smiles. "If I knew that, it'd be pretty easy. I think the answer is by really understanding myself, by knowing my goals, my limits—that sort of thing."

"How old are you?" I ask.

"I'm thirty-eight. I know, if I haven't found myself by now I ought to stop looking. But sometimes you only wake up late in life. I wasn't married until I was thirty."

"Do you like marriage?"

"After eight years of it, yes. It's the only way of life for me. I have a wonderful wife and two great little boys. It's like a closed circle, a magic circle." He smiles, as if he was embarrassed at his sentimentality. "That's the way marriage should be."

"What was your parents' marriage like?"

He seems surprised by the question. "They were good people, hard-working. My father ran a liquor store in Boston, and Mom worked with him." He smiles. "I should say she ran the business. Certainly she made all the decisions. My father was an immigrant; he came here from Ireland when he was thirteen and never got the old country out of his system—and he was a drinking man. The worst business in the world for him was the liquor store."

"Are they still alive?"

"No. Dad died when I was in the Army, and Mom just a few years ago. She was much younger than he. Hell, she was only sixteen when he married her."

"She died young."

He nods, and catches his lip with his teeth. "Very young. She had cancer, and it was a terrible time. My brothers and

I went through hell the last year of her life. Her own mother is still living."

"Was she happy with your father?"

Very quickly, he says, "Oh yes. Very, very happy—" He stops abruptly, and looks at me in surprise. "Why the hell am I saying that? They weren't happy at all. My father drank and she hated it. He was the kind of man who put her on a pedestal and worshiped her in a sloppy fashion, particularly when he was drunk. 'She's a saint, a saint, and I'm an animal,' and then all sorts of tears. Oh, Christ, it was a lousy marriage, a typical Irish marriage. He hated himself and never felt he measured up to her."

His blue eyes darken. "I don't know. I don't think I ever saw her as she really was. I saw her through my father's eyes, an angel, a saint, too good to touch—" He shrugs. "I saw every other woman the same way."

"What do you mean?"

"Just that. They were all too good to touch. Maybe that's what was the matter with me."

"That you put women on a pedestal?"

He leans forward intently. "I think so. I always liked women—as a kid, as a young man—but there was never any erotic arousal from women. I could never get sexually stimulated by a woman. I was a good Catholic in those days and I didn't see anything wrong with that. I just felt I was less sinful than my friends. I knew, at a very early age, that sex was dirty and ugly. I didn't need anyone to tell me that. Women didn't arouse me sexually, but men did."

Frowning a little, I ask, "But wouldn't the same logic work for homosexual sex? Surely by religious standards that's even dirtier."

Nodding, he says, "And by my family standards, too, but I think homosexual sex is a form of aggression against men, and I identified myself with women. I always fantasized myself in the feminine role, and that allowed me to control men."

"Did your mother control your father?"

He looks at me for a long moment, frowning a bit. Then, slowly, he nods. "Yes, in a way, for all his temper and drunken bouts, she could wind him around her finger. Maybe that's what I was after. It's funny, as a young boy I was very attracted to older men; there were spots in Boston where I could go and hang out and be picked up by them."

"Why older men?"

He strokes his mustache in a slightly nervous gesture. "I think I felt I could manipulate them better than men my own age. And it made the male-female relationship more clear-cut. I could be more of a woman with them, more flirtatious. It gave me a hold over them, and I enjoyed that." He shakes his head. "But there was no love involved. I never tied love into sex. In fact, once I got to know a man, once a relationship began to develop, I lost all erotic interest."

"How long did that go on?"

"All through my early teens." He frowns. "But I wasn't very satisfied with it. I wanted to relate to women, from the very beginning. That's the funny thing."

"If you wanted to, why couldn't you?"

"I guess you could say I was heterosexually impotent. I could have sexual relationships with men, but whenever I tried with my girl friends I was impotent."

"As a kid and a teen-ager, did you date girls?"

"Oh, yes. I went to all the church dances. I had girl friends I walked home from school, and some I kissed—it was a normal American boy's life, except that I could sneak downtown and have someone pick me up whenever I wanted to. Homosexually I was pretty knowledgeable. Heterosexually I was still a virgin."

"When did your homosexuality start?"

"I can't put a time on it. I know I was very young, in my early teens. It's funny, the incidents you remember. I have two older brothers, and my whole childhood was spent with them teasing me—at least that's how I remember it. One time I must have been particularly obnoxious because Bob, my middle brother, wanted to beat me up, but Dean, my older brother, said, 'Let's dress him up like a girl and take him downtown.' They kept threatening, but never did it."

"How did you feel?"

He smiles ruefully. "That's what's so funny, my reaction. I remember becoming terribly excited, sexually, and my heart began to race. I wanted it more than anything, but I knew I had to yell and protest and carry on so they'd think I didn't. But afterward I'd daydream about it, and even masturbate while I thought of it. In my fantasy world I began to think that the younger boys in the neighborhood, the ones I admired, would like me as a girl."

Leaning his chin on his fist, he looks across the garden. "You know, the biggest realization of my teens was that I could be liked by men for being a man, and I didn't have to be a girl, or effeminate."

"When did you have your first affair with a woman?"

He scratches his head. "In the Army, in Germany. I was on leave and I was spending the week at a fancy spa on a lake. I met Elsa there. She was a little older, maybe two years. I was about twenty-two. I was there with a bunch of gay guys who had picked me up while I was hitching, and she knew them and we had a few drinks together and swam, and then one afternoon the two of us were alone, and we went up to her room, very casually." He spreads his hands. "Just like that I went to bed with her."

"And there was no problem?"

"No impotence at all." He smiles delightedly.

"What do you think solved the problem?"

He considers that. "Maybe because I was so relaxed. Elsa knew I was gay, knew I was with a bunch of gay guys, and I didn't have to come on manly. I could be myself—and then it was in a very schmaltzy, German-romantic setting—

but there was no pressure. I think that was the most important thing."

"How did you feel afterward?"

"Oh, great, wonderful. As if I had solved the secrets of the universe. No, honest. I was really high. I thought, 'I've made it. I've really made it. and now I'm truly hetrosexual.' It was real euphoria!"

"Did it last?"

"Sure, as long as I was screwing Elsa. With the next girl I tried, I was impotent again. But I kept trying, and the next time it worked."

"Did you feel any guilt about your homosexuality?"

He shakes his head woefully. "Man, did I ever! My whole childhood was filled with guilt. I knew it would kill my parents. I knew I was sinning like crazy in the eyes of the church. I knew my friends would hate me if they found out, and to tell you the truth, I secretly believed I was going crazy."

"Crazy? Why?"

"Well, when we kids talked among ourselves we discussed that, how masturbation destroyed the mind, and how guys who had sex with other guys became degenerate. I knew I had already become that, only I wasn't sure if it was the masturbation or the homosexuality. Either way, I was a loser."

"Do you still feel guilty?"

He nods. "Yes, to this day, though I feel less guilty now. There's still some hanging on. You know, I think all the gay movements are great, Gay Liberation, Gay Pride—they're important because they give gay people a sense of pride in themselves. And that's what humans need to make it. I think if men want to love other men, or love men and women, they should. That's their business, not society's, and society's attitude is destructive."

"Destructive how?"

"Well, it destroys something in the man who goes against

it. It destroys his own sense of worth by saying he's doing wrong, by building up his guilt."

"Did your family know about your homosexuality or bisexuality?"

Frowning, he says, "No. My parents never did and my brothers and the rest of the family don't. I don't want them to. It's something they couldn't handle, and I don't have to prove anything to myself by telling them. Some of my close friends know, but no one at work. You can't tell by looking at me."

He smiles at that, and I nod. "No, you can't tell." And indeed you can't. Ellis's voice, appearance, and mannerisms are all male. He looks and acts like any other solid member of the establishment. "Did you see much of Elsa after that affair?" I ask.

"Some. When she could get to where I was stationed, but she was married, I found out, and pretty tied down."

"Did your sexual relationship to women change after that?"

"Yes, in the sense that I tried having sex more often, but I don't think at that point I was really a bisexual. I was a homosexual who was trying to have women, to become more heterosexual. I hate to put labels on things, to say this is homosexual, this bisexual, but it really was like that."

"When did you become bisexual?"

"Well, when I left the Army I went to law school, and that was a tough time. My mother couldn't help me. She was still trying to pull her life together after Dad's death, and finally my older brother, Dean, came through, and really put me through school, with an assist from the Army. Then, when I got into practice, I think I really conditioned myself into heterosexuality."

"Conditioned?"

He stretches and stands up. "Can I get you a drink? Some coffee?"

"That's fine." He brings out coffee and some biscuits and

lights a few bug candles. It's toward twilight, and the garden is very lovely in the yellow light of the candles.

I ask Ellis about conditioning again, and he explains. "Actually, I discovered the whole couples scene. It started with a girl I was trying to have an affair with. I was crazy about her and she turned me on sexually, but I was impotent with her, maybe because I was trying too hard, but she began to ask me all sorts of questions—we were in bed in a hotel in Taunton where she lived—and I finally told her about my homosexuality. Then she asked me if I would like a threesome, and the idea kind of excited me. I'd never had anything like that before. She called this friend of hers, a young, nice-looking guy, and he came over with a bottle and we hit it off. I mean, I liked him right off."

He pauses, and finally I ask, "What happened?"

"It was fantastic. I was aroused by him, and then I made love to her, and then he made love to her, and then the two of us—" His voice trails away. Finally he shakes his head. "Well, that was the beginning. I really got into that scene, and what happened was a gradual conditioning to the point where my impotence just about disappeared. Oh, I get it occasionally, but it doesn't bother me because I know it will be all right."

"Where did you find these couples?"

Evasively, he says, "Some by chance."

"By chance?" I sound doubtful.

"Well, to tell the truth, I advertised and answered ads, for a while, until I got into the swing of it. There's a whole network of couples who want another man as a partner. It's not hard to find them."

"And you enjoyed it?"

Again he strokes his mustache. "Enjoyed is too mild a word. You know, I think of that, sex with a couple, as a loving triangle."

"What do you mean?"

"Well, look, I think a good part of my homosexuality is a

search for my father. You know, a child grows up originally loving both his father and his mother. Then, all at once, at a certain age, he's not allowed to express any sexual feelings toward his father. He can still kiss his mother, but the society frowns on demonstrative feelings between men, and he must learn to curb what he feels for his father. With the loving triangle, I feel you get back to that. You're in a sexual situation with both your father and your mother. That's what's so wonderful about it."

"But that applies to the men in the situation," I point out. "What about the woman? She's with two fathers."

He smiles. "No situation is perfect. I suppose the ideal setup for a woman would be another couple, too. At any rate, it was wonderful for me. I could express both homosexuality and heterosexuality in a relaxed way. I think that was the key to overcoming my impotence, the ability to be open about being homosexual."

"But you never became completely heterosexual?"

"I didn't want to. What I wanted was to overcome my heterosexual impotence, and I did that. It took a couple of years of the couples scene, and then I was all right."

"You were able to function as a bisexual?"

He says, "Yes," hesitantly, then adds, "I don't really like the label bisexual. Maybe I just don't like to be identified as one."

"But you are one?"

"Oh, yes. I am, but maybe it's the fact that our society just doesn't accept it. There's something very wrong in most people's eyes about being bisexual."

"Worse than homosexual?" I ask doubtfully.

"Oh, yes. Maybe because bisexuality is really threatening."

"How do you mean, threatening?"

He leans back and spreads his hands. "Well, it's what they don't know. People know what queers are, but they don't understand that it's all right to open up emotionally and physically to anyone, male or female. They fear it."

"Why fear?"

"Because it's closer to being heterosexual." He leans forward intently. "Let's see if I can explain. A gay guy is pretty obvious, but a bi is more hidden, harder to spot. A bi is more like a straight, therefore it's more threatening."

"I'm not sure I understand."

"How can I explain?" Let's see—many men feel that homosexuality threatens them because they have homosexual elements in themselves. Right?"

I nod, and he goes on slowly. "Well, everyone has bisexual elements in them too. Men can love their fathers and brothers, and women their mothers and daughters and sisters . . . that's a part of the human condition. But society says *that* love is a no-no, so we're afraid of it. If someone comes along who feels that love and he looks like us and acts like us, he's a threat. See?"

"I think so." I hesitate. "But the love of a father for a son, or a mother for a daughter, isn't a sexual love."

He nods eagerly. "Yes. That's just it. Oh, there are sexual elements in that love, but let's leave them out. Just consider the love. The point is, it's part of the human condition to love others of the same sex. I'm married now, and I love my wife, deeply. Since my marriage my homosexual experiences have fallen off. I still will occasionally have a sexual encounter with a man, but more important, my emotional relationships to men, relationships that can be called bisexual, still continue. I relate to men sexually, which doesn't mean that I have to go to bed with them."

"I don't completely understand that."

"It's just that I can be attracted to a man sexually. I can appreciate him sexually, but I don't have to act out these feelings."

Puzzled, I ask, "What would keep you from acting them out? Society?"

He shakes his head with a hint of annoyance at my in-

ability to grasp his point. "No. Not society at all. It's preference. Oh, I still do, like I said, have sex with men sometimes, but I'm much more discriminating. It just isn't necessary, emotionally, because my emotional needs are satisfied
by my family. To go to bed with a guy just for the sake of
sex—that's O.K., but it isn't as important." He points his
finger to make it clear. "Look. I can have a close, intimate
friendship with a man with no sex involved, and as long as I
have the emotional support of my family, it would satisfy
my bisexual needs."

"There's a romantic element to that."

He chews one of the cookies thoughtfully. "Perhaps there
is, but is that so bad? I'm a child of the forties. I grew up
then, and I grew up with the movies of that period. Movies
were the major conditioning in my life, the romanticism of
the forties. Maybe I am romantic. So what?"

"When did you meet your wife?"

"After the Army, when I was about twenty-eight. I had
lived with a few women before that, in fact, at one time I
was engaged to be married, but I broke it off."

"Why?"

"She was a very pretty girl, but our relationship was
awfully bland. I met another girl and my feelings for her
were so strong and positive, so real, that by comparison the
girl I was engaged to was nothing. So I broke it off."

"Was that the girl you married?"

"No. It was a very quick but very alive affair."

"Have you ever had any kind of lasting relationship with
a guy?"

He shakes his head. "I couldn't live with a guy because
I'm too dependent on what society thinks; I always have
been. I don't think I could have made any sort of permanent
life with a man. I would want kids and acceptance in the
community—and there's my job. I work for a very conservative firm." He hesitates. "I could have a three-way relationship. I could live with a man and a woman."

"Have you ever done that?" I ask.

"Well—" He hesitates. "In a way, yes. My wife and I have lived with a close friend of mine, but there was no sexual relationship involved. It's funny. He lived with us for over a year, and we all got on well, but during that time I had no outside sexual encounters with men."

"Why not?"

"I didn't feel that I needed them. Jim and I had a good, satisfying emotional relationship." Stroking his mustache, he looks thoughtful. "Maybe that's what I've always been looking for, more than the sexual. I've always wanted the good sound emotional relationship with another man that I never had with my own father." He laughs. "Maybe that's the tie-in, looking for my father, for the image that feels satisfying and whole."

He's silent for a long time, and I become aware of the sharp sound of insect noises in the darkness. Finally he says, almost as a non sequitur, "My wife is very unlike my mother."

"Was your mother a strong woman?"

"I don't honestly know. She played on her weakness, but she ran things. I think it was less her being strong than my father being so miserably weak, so completely unable to stay sober, and such an animal when he drank!"

"What is your wife like?"

He sighs. "A very special person. Feminine, and sometimes boyish—strong. Many, many things." He shakes his head. "When I met her I had just broken off with a woman because we had—I should say I had—such problems of impotence. One of the beautiful things about my wife is that there's never been any impotence, not from the first time we spent together. We've never had any sexual problems."

"Is your wife bisexual?"

"Linda? No, she's monogamous."

"How does she feel about your bisexuality?"

"She thinks it's a stage I'm going to pass through. She's

completely heterosexual, and I don't think its possible for a
heterosexual person to understand bisexuality."

"But she accepts it in you?"

"More than accepts it. I think she's grateful for it."

"In what way."

"Well—" He shrugs. "In what it's made me."

"Made you?"

"It's added to our marriage."

Frowning, I ask, "But how? Not through involving others
with you sexually?"

"No. Actually, in a spiritual way. And she's also found
that some homosexual men can understand women better
than heterosexual men."

"Do you feel that you can?"

"Yes, and that's part of it. I share some of all women's
feelings. It has to do with being in touch with both the
masculine and the feminine sides of myself. Maybe that's
the real core of bisexuality."

"How is that?"

"Well, look, bisexuality doesn't really have to do with the
external parts of our bodies, the physical aspects of maleness and femaleness. It has to do with what's internal, with
what's in our minds. It has to do, in my case, with appreciat-
ing the part of me that's female as well as the part of me
that's male. It has to do with recognizing that I'm both at
the same time."

He laughs. "I'm on my soapbox," he says apologetically.

I say, "No. Please, I want to hear what you believe about
this."

Seriously, he goes on. "I believe that I am not my body.
I am my spirit, my essence, and by coincidence that essence
is existing in a male body and it has been trained by our
society to think male, to act male." He grins at me. "I go
on a lot about society. It's my favorite word. My colleagues
in our law firm tell me I'm a bleeding heart and that I'd free

every criminal because I insist the society has made him what he is."

"Do you believe that?"

"Sure. I don't believe in any inherent evil . . . any more than I believe in inherent maleness or femaleness. We learn to be what we are. I think our conceptions of ourselves in this twentieth century are very limited, that we are capable of being more than we are. Even in a business sense. I make twenty thousand dollars a year, and I have the capability of being male or female. I got off on the female start, maybe the wrong start—maybe the right—as a kid. I swung over to encompass both, and now, within myself, I can appreciate both. In that way I can identify more with my wife."

"And she senses this?"

"Oh, yes, and more than that. She has the same ability. I told you there are parts of her that are boyish. Well, she has a masculine, strong, aggressive side, but so have all women. Some hide it completely. Others let it dominate them. Basically, that's bisexuality."

"You have two boys. How do you plan to raise them in terms of their sexuality?"

"Right now they're children. One is five and the other is three. I wouldn't try and do anything but what we're doing, giving them lots of love and affection. I'll let them develop any way their nature takes them. If they arrive at bisexuality, O.K. That's the way they've come. If they become homosexual, that's their life. But I don't think they will."

"Why not?"

"Because I think homosexuality is a function of some love disturbance in childhood. I know mine was. There won't be any disturbance in the love we give them. My wife is a very loving mother, and I'm a loving father—and husband." He says this almost challengingly.

"What you've said," I try to choose my words carefully, "is that your growing up homosexual was a disturbed reaction. And yet you accept homosexuality."

"Accept it? Sure. I accept a lot of things I don't want for myself. I never wanted exclusive homosexuality. That's why I changed. Bisexuality is not homosexuality, any more than heterosexuality is bisexuality. They are different awarenesses of the human condition."

"When your sons are older, would you tell them about your bisexuality?"

"I don't know," he says slowly. But later, when he says good-bye, he comes back to this. "I don't think I'd tell my boys, but who knows. What's that Dylan song, *The Times They Are A-changing?* We're growing more toward openness and honesty and toward saying, 'Yes, this is how I am.' I wouldn't proselytize for bisexuality, but I would for allowing anyone to follow the path that seems natural to him." He shakes hands with me and adds, "There sure are a lot of possibilities. Multiple marriage, group marriage, open marriage. The culture is expanding. Maybe bisexuality is only part of that expansion."

Ellis said, "Maybe that's the real core of bisexuality. It has to do with being in touch with both the masculine and the feminine sides of myself." Much has been written about this since Freud noted we had a little of both within each of us. In spite of all of the learned journals and popular articles, most people are still afraid of the concept. Part of what the women's movement is saying is just that. Except for obvious physical features, most things we consider feminine appear to be culturally conditioned. There is a growing body of evidence that demonstrates that these feminine traits are taught to young children almost from the age of two months.

Men have a great deal of trouble accepting these feminine traits because they associate them with weakness. To be feminine is to be unable to protect yourself, to be unable to make decisions, and most important of all, to let your feelings dominate your decisions. It is this raw fear of feeling that I believe is the main component that disables men from accepting the softer sides of their personalities. To be rough is to be masculine, thus men handle tenderness by denying its existence. Whenever they feel it welling up, they compensate by becoming more and more rough or nonfeeling.

We have seen in most of our interviews that people are more afraid of bisexuality than they are of homosexuality. I believe this is because homosexuality is easier to discard by the majority of men. They know they do not want to be homosexual right off the bat. They would not even consider it. On the other hand, most men have had thoughts of touching another man's genitals or of hugging a close friend. Most of these men feel very guilty about having even one such thought. If they entertain the possibility of staying with women but yet "giving in" to this other feeling, it puts them in a terrible state of confusion.

One knows from prison stories how easy it is for men to turn sexually to other men when they are denied access to women. Also, the stories about men in the Navy have a great amount of truth in them. Most men placed in a position in which women are not available for long periods at a time will turn to homosexuality. In these cases, however, they are provided with a rationalization: There are no women. They also tell themselves that as soon as women became available, they will give up men. In most cases, this is certainly true. It does show that given certain conditions, men are capable of "going both ways."

There seems little doubt that Ellis's homosexual acts got their start from his family background. There was the mother who dominated everything, especially a weak father. It was the mother who had the power and the ability to punish for breaches of good behavior. The father gave the appearance of being the strong one, but underneath, Ellis knew it was his mother he had to deal with.

This type of family situation will tend to produce in men a fear of women. The fear leads to an excessive need to please the woman, first the mother, and then all other women. This reflects itself directly in sex in the form of impotency. If the desire to please is excessive, it extends to the sexual area. The man becomes afraid to try, which results in a lack of an erection. I have seen hundreds of men with this problem.

If we add to this the problem of putting the mother on a pedestal, then it becomes even harder to touch women sexually. In Ellis's case we have this double problem. He saw women as being too good for him and, at the same time, as punishing figures. When he had his first affair in which he could achieve a satisfactory erection, it was in circumstances where he felt perfectly comfortable and where he *knew* the woman accepted his deviant sexual behavior.

He saw himself in the feminine role, which allowed him to be in control. In his family background he saw that to lose this control was to be completely dominated. If he controlled men, he controlled himself.

As far as homosexual activities went, he said he never tied love and sex together. Further, once there was a romantic interest between himself and another man he tended to lose erotic interest. He sees his main interest in men as an attempt to find that kind of a father he never had—to have close contact with an accepting and understanding man. In this, he is certainly correct. Unfortunately, to understand something is not necessarily to change it. His homosexual actions did not stop simply because he understood some of the causal factors behind it.

Part of Ellis wants to re-create a family situation in which all the love that was not present in his own family as a child would be present. This is why he likes the idea of a "loving triangle." It is not so much the sex as the family part of it, with all the love he never saw as a child. Again, just to realize this is not to change it.

I was struck by the lack of any real discussion of his wife's feelings about his bisexual actions. I feel she was strongly opposed to it, but went along with it in the hope it would disappear. In Ellis's situation I would think that the homosexual activities would, over the years, gradually disappear as he became more and more secure in his relations with his own family. This does not mean his homosexual leanings might not come out in some other fashion, like being strongly involved with men's groups or with a boys' organization. This way he would get the emotional closeness he is looking for without the sexual participation.

The women in such cases are in a difficult position. It is difficult for the average women to visualize her husband making love to another man. When she thinks of him in bed with another woman, she has stereotyped feelings she can call forth—jealousy, anger, rage, throwing him out of the house. When it comes to homosexual sex, she is thrown into a state of anxiety because she doesn't know how she is "supposed" to act. It is also very difficult to talk about the problem with one of her friends because of the strong social prohibition in this area.

It is very difficult for women in this position to solve their problem without outside help. Some outside professional source should be selected, and both partners should consult with him. In many cases, the homosexual side is merely a passing action taken to meet some other need, and once that other need is filled, the homosexual activity will cease. Understanding on the part of the wife is essential. Certainly, if it turns out that the man or the wife is truly a bisexual without any conflicts or underlying unresolved problems, a totally different approach would have to be used. It would not be sufficient for the wife to wait it out. In this case, it would be essential to seek outside help.

In summary, I think Ellis has been through a stage of being bisexual that is rapidly coming to an end. His motivation for bisexuality has been recognized, and he has found ways of handling it short of sexual involvement.

11

Interview with
Dr. Wardell Pomeroy

I interview Dr. Wardell Pomeroy in his apartment in a large, new building on Manhattan's East Side. His office is a comfortable room—one wall lined with books, a large desk against the windows, and a couch and two Swedish, black leather lounge chairs taking up the rest of the space. An aquarium with tropical fish bubbles pleasantly in the background.

Dr. Pomeroy looks a robust man in late middle age. He has a shock of white hair and a pleasant, young face. Formerly a professor of psychology at the University of Indiana and a co-author of Kinsey's monumental work on human sexuality, Dr. Pomeroy has been associated with the Institute for Sex Research and is now in private practice in New York City. The bulk of his work involves counseling sexually disturbed couples.

How would you define bisexuality?

Dr. Pomeroy: I would say a bisexual is someone who rates two, three, or four on the Kinsey heterosexual-homosexual rating scale.

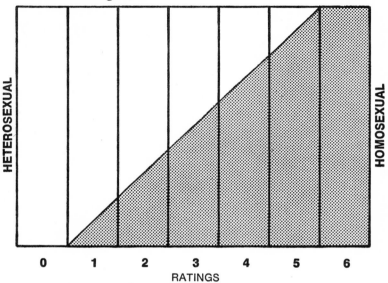

RATINGS

Heterosexual-homosexual Rating Scale

*Based on both psychologic reactions
and overt experience, individuals rate as follows:*

0. Exclusively heterosexual with no homosexual
1. Predominantly heterosexual, only incidentally homosexual
2. Predominantly heterosexual, but more than incidentally homosexual
3. Equally heterosexual and homosexual
4. Predominantly homosexual, but more than incidentally heterosexual
5. Predominantly homosexual, but incidentally heterosexual
6. Exclusively homosexual

Could you explain that scale?

Dr. Pomeroy: It contains seven classifications, from zero to six. Those who fall into zero are exclusively heterosexual with no homosexual psychological reactions or overt experiences. Those who fall into six are exclusively homosexual. The other categories range from predominantly heterosexual with only incidental homosexual experience to predominantly homosexual with incidental heterosexual experience. Category two is predominantly heterosexual, but more than incidentaly homosexual. Three is equally heterosexual and homosexual, and four is predominantly homosexual with more than incidental heterosexuality.

How many people fall into those categories, two, three, and four?
Dr. Pomeroy: Off hand, I would say we're talking about ten per cent of all men and five per cent of all women. That's fifteen per cent of the total population.

That's a tremendous number of people.
Dr. Pomeroy: Yes, but another way of looking at it is in terms of how a person defines himself. A man may be a two on the Kinsey scale, but think of himself as heterosexual. He's defining himself.

But in terms of reality he's a bisexual, isn't he?
Dr. Pomeroy: What I've been fighting, and what Kinsey fought, is the concept that a man is either gay or straight. People have always thought in terms of those two extremes, and have put people into those two categories. Now we have another category, bisexuality. I prefer to think in terms of a continuum from zero to six. If within the continuum you can speak of homesexuality and heterosexuality, then you can also logically speak of bisexuality.

Is there a psychological definition of bisexuality?
Dr. Pomeroy: Well, I think if you consider the man who is overtly a zero on the Kinsey scale, but who has homosexual dreams when he masturbates and is turned on

by seeing an attractive man on the street, you'd have to say that psychologically he's a two or three. Is he bisexual? Overtly he's not, but psychologically he is.

But you are speaking of two types of definition.
Dr. Pomeroy: Yes. Usually the overt and the psychological follow each other. Your psyche is turned on by what you do overtly, but there are exceptions. Consider a married man who only has intercourse with his wife. Psychologically, however, he might be a five or six who is blocked from outside sex. However, this is an exception.

In marriages where the man is bisexual and has outside affairs, how successful have the couples been in staying together?
Dr. Pomeroy: If the man is a two he doesn't have much trouble, but if his homosexual component is equal to, or greater than his heterosexual component, say a three or a four, there just won't be enough stimulation on a heterosexual level to sustain the marriage.

How do you place an individual on this scale?
Dr. Pomeroy: By taking a complete sexual history, including all his overt behavior. We pose a whole series of questions about his psyche, his masturbations, his dreams, whether he's aroused by men or women or both. We find out if he looks at a picture of a penis when he masturbates, or a vagina, or if he's turned on by his own penis. After a couple hours of such intensive questioning, you can usually arrive at a placement. The same applies for women, of course, but the questions would differ.

When a married man is in the two area, how does he usually resolve his marriage?

Dr. Pomeroy: Usually the wife doesn't know about it. The most common pattern is to continue the marriage without telling her and have surreptitious homosexual behavior on the side. Usually, when the wife learns about it, it becomes very upsetting to her and breaks up the marriage.

What is the basis for the wife's upset?

Dr. Pomeroy: She's responding to the taboos that our society imposes, that such behavior is evil, bad, sick, neurotic. Wives, more than husbands, feel this is wrong and that they have been betrayed.

In many of the married bisexuals we interviewed, we found that they would be satisfied with one woman, but not one man. They needed multiple homosexual contacts. Why does this happen?

Dr. Pomeroy: Well, let's turn this around into heterosexuality and consider the married man who has outside affairs with women.

But that doesn't really apply. This is a bisexual man, not having affairs with other women, just other men.

Dr. Pomeroy: In general, homosexuality tends to be more promiscuous. Such men are usually interested in variety. The fact that he wasn't getting variety in his sexual life with his wife might account for his interest in males.

But surely a man can find variety with a woman.

Dr. Pomeroy: But there is the additional problem of the marriage. If he turned to women, he would be unfaithful.

You mean he makes the psychological distinction, I am not unfaithful with a man, but I am with a woman?

Dr. Pomeroy: That's one of the dynamics of the situation. I have a patient who isn't married, but sleeps with one girl friend. However, he has many one-night stands with men. I would put him into a four category on the scale. What I'm working on is to get him into a long-standing relationship with one man, which would pull him down toward three. He doesn't want to be exclusively heterosexual, but he would like to fall in the middle of the bisexual group.

Do you think that bisexuality is a viable way of life?
Dr. Pomeroy: For some people it is, but only for a minority.

You speak of bringing men down from homosexuality toward heterosexuality. Does the same apply to women?
Dr. Pomeroy: There seems to be more lability with women. With a man, you can get a patient who falls into the six category on the scale and you can, after therapy, after a great deal of therapy, get him down to a five, or a four, or even lower, but you never seem to get him below two. Women are different. I have seen a woman change, in the course of a few months, from six to zero and from zero to six.

Is this because a woman can function heterosexually, even if she is homosexual, simply because there is no physical function to before? A man, however, must achieve an erection before he can have a heterosexual affair.
Dr. Pomeroy: Yes, but aside from the act of sexual penetration, I'm considering the psychological response. Women shift psychologically.

What would account for this, culturally?
Dr. Pomeroy: I suppose, the psychological differences between men and women. I don't believe that women are as affected by psychological stimuli as men are. Per-

haps it's cultural, but animal studies seem to indicate that there are genetic differences.

Do you find that gay people as well as straight are antagonistic toward bisexuality?

Dr. Pomeroy: Yes, but we have found an even stranger response. In interviewing people who profess to be zero, we often find it's like pulling teeth to get them to admit to being one or two. On the other end of the scale, however—and this is what surprised us—gay people who admitted to being six were extremely reluctant to admit to five or four.

What is the reluctance due to?

Dr. Pomeroy: They're locked into the concept that a person is either straight or gay, either/or.

You've interviewed swinging couples. Have you found that this has accelerated any homosexual activity?

Dr. Pomeroy: It has on the part of the women, and I have spoken to some men who were so threatened by the homosexual implication that they got out of the swing altogether. But you get another phenomenon, married men who arrange to have their wives have sex with another man while they watch. Afterward they immediately have cunnilingus with their wives. Most of them aren't aware of the homosexual overtones, of getting at the male semen in their wives' vaginas.

Would you say that bisexuality is the wave of the future?

Dr. Pomeroy: I don't see that at all. It's too complicated a thing, psychologically, I mean. Take two couples living together. Sex is the easiest part of it. It's complicated enough for two people to get along, imagine what it's like with four.

Have you run into this in your practice?

Dr. Pomeroy: Yes. I have a patient who had his wife and girl friend both living with him. At first it seemed to him the best of all possible worlds. But if you think of it as a triangle with him on top, and his wife at one base and his girl friend at the other, there was nothing to connect the two bases, and the whole thing fell apart. The two women just had nothing in common, except him.

Could you have such a triangle if the two women were involved sexually?

Dr. Pomeroy: That would work much better from some standpoints, but remember, it isn't just the sex that's a problem. The basic problem lies in three people living together. It's hard enough for two, but when you have a third—well, think of the inlaws, the money, the chores, and on and on.

One of the men we interviewed had a good relationship going with a man and a woman, on a lasting basis. It would seem that this is the logical route for a bisexual. Is it common?

Dr. Pomeroy: It's not common. Look, if there weren't the institution of marriage, why confine yourself to two people? Why not have other occasional affairs? Marriage is really the factor that ties people down.

Would you consider bisexuality normal?

Dr. Pomeroy: How do you judge normality? Statistically it's abnormal. Biogenetically it's normal. Morally it's abnormal and legally it's abnormal, but socially it's normal.

Why do you feel it's socially normal?

Dr. Pomeroy: My definition of socially normal is something

that doesn't harm society. Rape and molesting children are abnormal. I can't see many other sexual practices that are.

Do you think bisexuality is an inroad to the collapse of marriage?
Dr. Pomeroy: Not at all.

We found some couples who felt that bisexuality brought their marriages together by making them more trusting and open.
Dr. Pomeroy: This might be true for about five per cent of marriages. The same could be said of swinging. They are definitely helpful, but only in a limited number of marriages.

Do you think, from what you've seen, that bisexuality is really the acting out of other problems?
Dr. Pomeroy: I don't really see that. You know, you can act out problems heterosexually. If you follow that line of reasoning you can conclude that sex itself is only a cover-up for other fears or problems.

Do you consider bisexuality a part of the new sexual revolution?
Dr. Pomeroy: It's not at all new. It's been around for a number of years, and it's been accepted in many cultures, by many North African cultures, by Turkey, some Buddhist cultures. We tend to forget that the culture of our Old West, the cowboy culture, was rampant with homosexuality. They despised effeminacy, the appearnce of homosexuality, but not the act. Of course, women were in short supply there, and it was more bisexuality than homosexuality.

Do you think that as the society loosens up bisexuality will increase?

Dr. Pomeroy: It may in the short run, but I don't think it will as a long-term thing. There'll be an apparent increase due to the fact that there'll be less guilt and fear about it. It's out in the open. It's discussed, and people may be a bit more open about practicing it.

But could the openness push people into practicing it?

Dr. Pomeroy: People just don't change that easily. Studies done on the effect of the Kinsey reports showed that people were more relaxed about what they did, but they did the same things they did before the reports came out.

What forces make a man bisexual—or a woman?

Dr. Pomeroy: I think that's the wrong question. You should ask why isn't everybody bisexual? What keeps people from bisexuality? Genetically, you would expect that everyone was.

Not really. We've evolved genetically with two sexes for reproduction. You would expect heterosexuality to be the main stream of sexuality.

Dr. Pomeroy: I think you're ignoring the fact that sex is fun.

Isn't that hooked onto sex by nature to ensure reproduction?

Dr. Pomeroy: Perhaps, but the fun is still there. Even animals display a great deal of homosexual behavior.

So, genetically, you feel bisexuality is normal. Would you say that if people were free of their cultural impediments, the society would be bisexual?

Dr. Pomeroy: It would still be more heterosexual, and that's

what you see in the cultures where bisexuality is accepted.

But if everyone were free to be bisexual, why would the
predominance of heterosexuality remain?

Dr. Pomeroy: Anatomically, sex is better between a man
and a woman. You can't forget that. And of course you
have the bond of children and the family. I suppose,
too, there is the contrast between the sexes, the soft
breast of the woman against the hard chest of the man
—that, too, is a factor.

Do the bisexuals you have interviewed or treated have problems with their children?

Dr. Pomeroy: Like the swingers, they cover it up completely. Sometimes they worry that their children will
be this way, but usually they can leave their children
out of their bisexual life.

Does bisexuality work any better when the wife accepts it?

Dr. Pomeroy: There are different degrees of acceptance. If
she accepts it completely, it may be a tremendous relief
in the marriage and a growing experience for both of
them, but again it comes back to how homosexual the
husband is. It's easier if he's a two than if he's a three
or four.

Easier in the eyes of the wife?

Dr. Pomeroy: No. Easier in terms of their ability to get
along.

But wouldn't a three, right in the middle, be someone who
could be in love with his wife as well as other men? Or does
a three really exist?

Dr. Pomeroy: The man in the middle? He does only in the

sense of a fine balancing act. For instance, he may like a woman's breasts better than a man's flat chest, but a penis better than a vagina. He may like the wife to do housework, but still like to go out with the boys.

Aren't you forgetting that you can love either sex in terms of the person? If you're a three, won't it depend on the man or woman you meet?
Dr. Pomeroy: Yes. That's very often true.

So many psychiatrists have come out to say that bisexuality is sick, but from what you've said, you obviously don't feel this.
Dr. Pomeroy: No, I don't. As for other psychiatrists, they have a right to their own problems.

But don't you have to define "sick"? Isn't "sick" what the society doesn't accept? If that's true, at this time bisexuality is certainly sick.
Dr. Pomeroy: I think you're right. There are even parts of the society that insist a full-fledged homosexual is O.K., but a bisexual isn't. Again, there are many people brought up in a rigid moral atmosphere who object to bisexuality on that basis alone. Yes, we can easily fall into the trap of thinking that anyone who doesn't believe as I do is masking something.

To get back to the question I asked before. What early conditioning could lead to bisexuality?
Dr. Pomeroy: Well, there are many children who get involved with both sexes but don't grow up bisexual. What keeps them from it? I think the mother-father relationship is a complicated, complex, and multifaceted possibility of how they develop. Some say a close-binding mother and an absent father are respon-

sible in eighty-five per cent of homosexuals, but what about the others? Or the fifty to sixty per cent of heterosexuals who had the same mother-father relationship?

Do you think that given a specific type of personality, certain environmental factors will pull it toward homosexuality, while the same factors will not affect a different personality?
Dr. Pomeroy: That's probably the answer toward which we're going to go, but we don't know what those factors are.

Do the same factors apply to the bisexual?
Dr. Pomeroy: We haven't really worked this out. They have tried to study twins and homosexuality, and one study showed a higher percentage of homosexuality in identical twins than in fraternal, and a higher percentage in fraternal than in brothers and sisters, but it wasn't a good study and the results are open to question. I haven't leaned too strongly toward the genetic theory in the past, but I'm a bit more open about it now. One thing that fascinates me about homosexuality is what I call the false positives. Men who act effeminate but are very definite heterosexuals, zeros on the Kinsey scale.

There is obviously a great deal more research to be done in this area. Masters and Johnson are doing some, and there are hormonal studies in progress—I feel it's still an untapped field, but a fascinating one.